Patrick Marnham is author of eleven b
Wasn't Maigret, Fantastic Invasion, S
of Diego Rivera and Jean Moulin. Hi
seven languages and he has won the T ard,
the Marsh Biography Award and was no dgar Allen Poe
Award in 1994. He started his career as a reporter on *Private Eye* and has contributed to many newspapers including *The Times,* the *Daily Telegraph,* the *Observer,* the *New York Times,* the *Washington Post* and the *Los Angeles Times.* He has been literary editor of *The Spectator*, was the first Paris correspondent of *The Independent*, has worked as a BBC scriptwriter and broadcaster and as a special correspondent and war reporter. *Road to Katmandu* was his first book.

Tauris Parke Paperbacks is an imprint of I.B.Tauris. It is dedicated to publishing books in accessible paperback editions for the serious general reader within a wide range of categories, including biography, history, travel, art and the ancient world. The list includes select, critically acclaimed works of top quality writing by distinguished authors that continue to challenge, to inform and to inspire. These are books that possess those subtle but intrinsic elements that mark them out as something exceptional.

The colophon of Tauris Parke Paperbacks is a representation of the ancient Egyptian ibis, sacred to the god Thoth, who was himself often depicted in the form of this most elegant of birds. Thoth was credited in antiquity as the scribe of the ancient Egyptian gods and as the inventor of writing and was associated with many aspects of wisdom and learning.

ROAD TO KATMANDU

PATRICK MARNHAM

TAURIS PARKE
PAPERBACKS

For John Perkins

Published in 2005 by Tauris Parke Paperbacks
An imprint of I.B.Tauris and Co Ltd
6 Salem Road, London W2 4BU
175 Fifth Avenue, New York NY 10010
www.ibtauris.com

In the United States of America and in Canada distributed by
Palgrave Macmillan, a division of St Martin's Press,
175 Fifth Avenue, New York, NY 10010

First published in 1971 by Macmillan London Ltd
Copyright © 1971, 2005 Patrick Marnham

Cover image 'Stupa in Kathmandu' © Michael Freeman/CORBIS

ISBN 1 84511 017 X
EAN 978 1 84511 017 8

A full CIP record for this book is available from the British Library
A full CIP record for this book is available from the Library of Congress

Library of Congress Catalog Card Number: available

Printed and bound in India by Replika Press Pvt. Ltd.

ROAD TO KATMANDU

— *travelled by 'a bunch of zombies like us'*

'. . . how am I to face the odds
Of man's bedevilment and God's?
I, a stranger and afraid
In a world I never made.
They will be master, right or wrong;
Though both are foolish, both are strong.'
                          A. E. Housman *Last Poems*

Contents

INTRODUCTION TO 2005 EDITION

The road to Katmandu has long since been cut and the journey described in these pages has not been possible for many years. One by one, in a macabre demonstration of domino theory, the countries identified in the 60s as centres of spiritual liberation and hedonism became no-go areas or war zones.

The process started in the 1970s when the Turkish and Iranian governments introduced the death penalty for drug trafficking. Then, the Shah's imperial Persia became Iran and went to war for eight years in the 1980s, while in Afghanistan the invading Soviet army devastated the north and west of that primitive land. In 1968, when I travelled through Afghanistan, the Soviet and US embassies were competing with each other to provide the country with a single modern highway. At the time I thought of the hordes to follow; of the commercial and cultural destruction that threatened this fragile landscape. It has not happened. Instead, Al-Qaeda and its supporters have turned the Afghan-Pakistan border into their hinterland while in Nepal the Maoist guerrillas kidnap foreign travellers and the army is said to have lost control of the roads leading into Katmandu. Is there anything as threatening as innocence? The question has to be asked when one considers the havoc wreaked on so many Asian countries following the impact of the western search for Nirvana.

For overlanders the loss was irreplaceable. When the East could only be reached by a slow and sometimes painful overland trek, the journey became part of that enriching experience. And it had a powerful attraction for Arcadians, it was a journey back through time. Across the Bosphorus, the last major watercourse until the Ganges, lay Asia with its huge skies and empty plains soaking up the traffic until there was nothing, few villages, fewer roads, little sign of human activity, just wind and birds and stars. The further you went the stronger grew the conviction that you had at last tumbled over the edge so that no one in the world knew where you were. And that was perhaps the most liberating experience of all.

I will never search for those hills or tracks again but the memory of them recalls the days when life stretched ahead, far beyond the horizon, when time was too vast to measure, when mistakes were of such little importance since there was so much space in which to repair them. I can still see the way in which the new road curved downhill as we left Refayihe, and the bend where our escort of schoolchildren finally gave up. I can still see the light changing behind my arm, chased by clouds, as I lay back in an open pickup and we raced towards Yozgat, accompanied by a small man with a thick moustache, dressed in sacking who smelt of saffron, and a harmonica player attempting 'Billy Boy'. I still wonder what happened to Aziz, the young merchant of Herat, with his state-of-the-art Olivetti Lettera 22 (a portable typewriter) and his easy friendship and his excellent English. Did he survive it all; the Soviet invasion, the Taliban and the 'Can-do, shoot first' gunships of the US Marines? Does Aziz still smile in welcome when he sees a strange face from the West?

In 1968 Istanbul, a city synonymous with Levantine decadence, provided the perfect farewell to Europe. With the souks and hamams surrounding its filthy cheap hotels it retained some of its faded splendour. And its cynical, amused population were far too preoccupied with their traditional pleasures to be more than amused by the passing cavalcade. I travelled with Perkins, my friend, to whom this edition is dedicated. We knew nothing about each other before we left, and it didn't matter since all that was worth knowing lay in how we would deal with the days ahead. Looking back now I think I went too fast for Perkins. He would have liked to spend a lot more time in all the best places, and of course he was right. Wherever we turned he could see possibilities that were more promising than my restless need to investigate what lay around the next bend.

We set out at the end of May, on a day when the Latin Quarter in Paris had been burning for four weeks. The fact that not even the French in the Gulhane showed much interest in those events was the measure of our innocence. The hippies and vagabonds of the 60s sought no conventional political revolution. When we reached the Nepalese border the guards presented us with lapel pins bearing a portrait of King Mahendra one of whose sayings was, 'Student politics are gruesome'. 'What is the aim and object of all this movement?', the Indian army officers demanded, and put so succinctly it was hard to know how to reply. Perhaps it was just that; to move away from the world of 'aim and object'. While the idealists of our generation were embracing the intolerant discipline of the theory of surplus value we wanted to find a reason for postponing commitment; a way of keeping possibilities open, of not being forced to decide who you wanted to be.

The people who lived on the road had more urgent problems. Six weeks after our journey there was a catastrophic earthquake in eastern Iran, and in the eleven years that followed 60,000 Iranians died in similar events. Prompted by hardship, the East's response to our quest was not long in coming. It was expressed in the gentle mockery of Gita Mehta who wrote *Karma Cola*, in the spiked cocktails of Charles Sobhraj who killed hippies for pleasure and in the officially authorised violence portrayed in *Midnight Express*. Innocence provoked contempt. What followed was much worse. Did the hippies bear some indirect responsibility for the Ayatollahs or the Taliban? They certainly earned little respect from the communities they travelled among, even if their personal responsibility was nil. Can people who eat so badly that they can no longer sell their own blood be held responsible for anything? But there was exhilaration as well as degradation in that journey and despite the desperate circumstances of some who travelled, what endures for me is the power of their optimism.

My own journey was never intended to provide the material for a book, which is why I eventually wrote a partly fictional account. In a way, Rat, the main fictional character is also the most authentic. You can control a character you create and invest him with a measure of truth; the truth that endures when diligent reportage has been reduced to a series of blurred snapshots.

AUTHOR'S NOTE

The journey described here was of the type foreseen by Evelyn Waugh in a partly prophetic introduction to his book of assorted travels, *When The Going Was Good* (1945): 'My own travelling days are over, and I do not expect to see many travel books in the near future ... there is no room for tourists in the world of "displaced persons" ... the very young, perhaps, may set out like the *wandervögel* of the Weimar period; lean, lawless, aimless couples with rucksacks, joining the great army of men and women without papers, without official existence, the refugees and deserters, who drift everywhere today between the barbed wire.'

The people who hitched to Katmandu (and are doubtless still doing so, despite the usual reports of official prohibitions) seem to me to be of this sort, displaced persons, aimless couples without papers. They are ill-suited to play the role which they are conventionally given; that of proletarian playboys, outriders of a modern sub-culture, who intend, mainly through will-power, to end injustice and rule the world. For the most part they have chosen to be the sole inhabitants of private worlds, and their aspirations will not be found in the bazaars of the international youth movement, or of the global underground or any other such tentative organisations.

The new *wandervögel* have many reasons for their restlessness. Perhaps the one belief that they share is that in a different place they will become different persons. Like Hazlitt they have an innocent faith in the idea that by going on a journey they will escape themselves. This is a proposition so hopeful that few might care to reject it out of hand. The experiences of those I met with on this road suggest nonetheless that it is false, and that all too often such journeys away from oneself lead nowhere.

Few of the characters in this book exist as real individuals. But I hope that many of those who have travelled on the road to Katmandu will recognise some of the incidents. One of the journeys described was instigated by John Anstey, the Editor of the *Daily Telegraph Magazine*, to whom my thanks are due.

Patrick Marnham

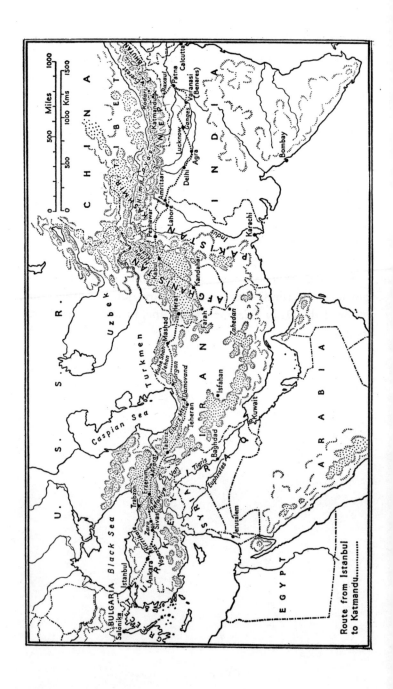

Route from Istanbul to Katmandu..........

I The Tent

All through that night the hotel lobby filled with travellers. They gathered like swallows on a wire and chattered and preened and dared, and as the evening passed and more new-comers limped off the road from Salonika the flock became more excited. They huddled closer, their boasts grew wilder and their clamour spilled out into the narrow streets.

Glen retailed the latest news from Greece. Last week he had been selling blood, and while he was lying on the bed with a needle in his arm the door of the clinic burst open and an old Orthodox priest who had fallen ill outside stag-gered in. The old priest had taken one look round the weird scene, thrown up his arms, and died. 'Poor old priest,' said Glen. 'Gets as far as the hospital, and the last thing he sees is a bunch of zombies like us.' He was still brooding about this. Priests occupied a special place in his mythology. They were displaced idols, fathers who had failed but they deserved his affection for trying.

Pete had also come in from Salonika; he was preoccupied with another priest. Did we know that there was a town in north India where the Dalai Lama was living now? He just existed in this town surrounded by a few faithful Tibetans and held court and meditated. And if anyone wanted an audience with him they only had to find the town and ask. Pete knew of someone who had had an audience with the Lama and in the middle of it the holy one had levitated and floated round the room, still giving his audience. 'Wasn't that cool?' Not even the Pope levitated during an audience.

Rat had been there the longest of all. He had arrived during the winter when the hotel was still empty. The Gulhane was a small hotel in the poorest part of Istanbul, but for a few pennies a night people could sleep on the roof, beneath the polythene tent which the proprietor had rigged up to keep the rain off. Outside it might be pouring down, with a gusty wind blowing in from the Bosphorus and the polythene blowing with it, slapping and cracking in the darkness, letting in quite a bit of the rain, just failing to collapse; from a neighbouring house it would be a stretch of grubby polythene, whipping in the wind, giving off a slight glow, letting out a snatch of singing now and then. But inside, in the warm, it was the Tent, on a roof right under the Blue Mosque, among the last buildings in Europe; the place you stayed if you had no money.

For most of those who reached it the Gulhane was a destination, the house furthest east, halfway home again. But nobody wanted to admit this. To say that they had come far enough and were now turning back was shameful. The Gulhane, after all, was no sort of a prize in the quest of these displaced persons, fugitives from the social and economic wars of Europe and north America.

The people who stayed in the Gulhane were deserters; either on the run, or in search of the way of life which as children they had known they would be able to make for themselves. Most of them had barely left school and already they needed another chance; they were searching for a way out of the trap which their lives had become. And so, like men in a panic, they ran, it did not matter in which direction; as long as they were on the move there was hope. And as they ran they listened – just in case there was anywhere to run to. In the Gulhane it was said that that place was east, anywhere east, but especially Katmandu, which was as high and cool as you wanted, and where there were Buddhas and butterflies and hash. Even a deserter could be free.

Rat had seen some changes in these months. The season was starting now, the place was filling up. The police were raiding for drugs again, and there were several dozen over-landers in the town jail as a result. There was a feeling of tension in the Tent just now: the police seemed to call only when it was worth their while, and people were talking of an informer.

One man in particular was under suspicion. A weasel of an Austrian, small, with flaming red hair and an endlessly dis-charging nose, who had a zealous aggression towards strangers. But he did not aim his aggression truly, this weasel, he lost his temper at the wrong times and with the wrong people, and as a result those who had had a genuine experience of suspicion and mistrust, mistrusted him. He said that his name was Thor. The trouble with Thor was that he was an amateur hash trader, and it was fairly clear that in a city like Istanbul an amateur hash trader had no chance of staying out of jail. Yet here he was scampering around without a care in the world, apparently unmolested by the police. Now, when the little man threatened and blustered in the Tent, all but the newest arrivals felt that they could afford to laugh at him. He was an informer and sooner or later he would be shown to be one; until then he could be laughed at.

Rat was also involved with the police, though in not quite so intimate a fashion as Thor. When he first arrived in Istan-bul Rat was accosted by the big Italian known as Louis who was hoping to employ him on the heroin trade route between

Istanbul and Geneva, driving a large car with packed sides. This was an assignment which Rat was more than a little anxious to avoid, but he could see no way out of it. Big Louis seemed to be able to make life very unpleasant anywhere between the Blue Mosque and the German border. He had an arrangement with many of the Customs guards and he had an even better arrangement with more of the civilians. And Rat did not have the money for an airfare. So like a lot of the people in the Gulhane he had discovered that his life had become a trap. He could not make his way home overland. There were wise men who had told him that there was no such thing as a second chance, that he had made his bed and must lie on it and similar depressing reflections, but Rat ignored them. He needed another chance and it still seemed to him that if he needed something he would eventually get it. So here he was, just looking around.

Two days earlier a Swiss boy had walked into the Tent carrying a fishing rod. The fact of this tatty wanderer being Swiss was already encouraging, and the fact that he lived off his skill as a fisherman was more so. He carried nothing but his rod and a shoulder bag and he said that the rivers of Bulgaria and Yugoslavia were unlicensed and a fishing paradise. As confirmation there was the smell of his clothes.

To sweeten him up Rat had taken him to Yenner's, which was a small cafe nearby which Yenner had allowed to reach such a state of decrepitude that his only clients were now those on the road. 'Welcome to Yenners,' he had written on the peeling wall and beneath the obligatory portrait of Ataturk another hand had scribbled, 'Hell is empty, all the devvils are here'. A coke cost sixty kurus, cigarettes were fifty kurus a pack. You could sit there all day eating bread for eighty kurus. Here the Swiss had gorged himself on stuffed aubergines. Opposite a young Turk pulled an American girl's hair, though without much energy or enthusiasm. The girl's two friends looked on. One was stabbing fleas with a spittled finger and then truncating them with his thumb nail. For the time being this took priority over any other business.

It was a public holiday that day, and the Swiss was so disgusted with all the military bands that he set out on the very same afternoon for Teheran. So Rat was alone again.

Walking round the city after he had gone the Rat envied the Swiss. As he passed the money lenders gave out their exchange rate chants to the tourists and assailed him. 'Hasheesh, hasheesh, fresh, sweet, green. You wan sell your watch?' The tourists hurried by, thankful for a break but anxious to put a good distance between them and the Rat. Tourists were frightened of Rat. They never knew when this private in the army of the unkempt was likely to spring up and do something that might focus the world's attention on them. That was what really worried the average tourist. The thought that he might have to draw attention to himself by reacting visibly to a situation, was enough to paralyse him with fear. There was a possibility that he would have to leave the protective camouflage of his party and become just a person in the street. And could he speak the language of the other persons in the street? If he got lost could he ask a policeman? Which ones were the policemen anyway? It seemed to Rat that the average package tourist was already a very nervous man, and the possibility, in a city like Istanbul, was that he was also a guilty one. Everywhere he looked were the miserably poor, picking up sticks, begging him for food, defiling everything they touched, including, most particularly, his newly laundered sleeve.

To cheer himself up he went and sat on the steps of the Blue Mosque and watched the guardian turning away the sleek female tourists for the gleaming indecency of their uncovered arms; but today this did not have its usual soothing effect, for after a while the guardian chased him away too, and then Rat began to feel like a pariah. Yenner's seemed too much like a bolt hole so Rat went to the Pudding Shop instead. Here the proprietor still had a thriving Turkish trade, and for only fourpence halfpenny and a barrage of abuse from the assembled natives you could gorge yourself on his slurpy chocolate pudding, hot and black and sweet. The proprietor was sensible enough to let the girls eat it free, so there were always plenty of girls about, and the tables down the opposite wall of the cafe were packed with the young men of the quarter – and blades from smarter quarters too for the Pudding Shop was a popular place to go slumming. The men in crisp white shirts and tight silk trousers flocked in and hungrily watched the hungry girls. They knew they were not wasting their time, these men, for was it not well known that this was riff-raff from the west? And had not this riff-raff reached the level of decadence where it was unable even to guard its own women? As Rat walked back to the Tent the blades were packing into big old Fords and roaring up and down the road, leaning out in fours to shout insults at any weirdie who chanced their way.

So, a little later on that crowded wet night, Rat started to think about the road. He talked to Gunther who sat by the wall all day writing in a small notebook bound in cedar wood. Gunther was German, but he spoke fair English and French and he wrote about the atomic armageddon which he knew was on the way. He knew about it because he had dreamt it, and his dreams foretold the future. He had given up morphine because it interfered with his dreams, and now he could remember them better and write them down. Gunther was writing the story of his life; about the small town near Dachau where he used to live, about the guest house there which his mother owned, and the river nearby where he swam as a child. It had been fun to take the foreign soldiers to the river and point out to them the best parts in which to swim – just below the sewage outlet. At the time it had seemed a mild revenge for a childhood marked by their condescension and courtesy; now he was not so sure.

Rat knew that Gunther would not be making the journey east. He had reached the Tent and there he would stay. He had tried to think a path through the confusion. But it was like trying to cut adamant with wax. 'The bible is wrong,' said Gunther. 'I know where Allah should fit into it. Allah is the will, and God will punish us for every time we follow the will. There is no escape from God, not even fantasy. Because God always has a better fantasy of his own.' Nothing really distracted Gunther; just occasionally he caught sight of some of his fellow residents. 'Look at that clown,' he said, 'what a drag he makes of his days.'

That clown was sitting with his back to another wall, the centre of an admiring group, robed in the bric-a-brac of three eastern religions. He sucked on the broken bottle neck he used as a pipe for the burning drug. He was not altogether unsatisfied with his appearance. The clown would not be making it to the east either. He too had come far enough.

But there were others who had been there, and others again who were likely to go. Thor said that he had been to Kabul, and this accounted in part for his steady private supply of hash. Thor said that that was where he had met his girl, a lady who shared his flaming red hair and who added to this an extraordinary transparency of skin; the more romantic of the overlanders believed her to be his sister.

Gunther had just estimated that there were at present five of his friends in jail as a result of the police raids, and Thor had begun to sense that he might be connected with this calculation, and to prepare his retreat accordingly. Retreat was Thor's best plan. He had no friends in the Tent, and his 'sister' would be of very little help to him. She had a sharp tongue and there were those who felt that they had a score to settle with her as

well. But for Rat Thor could wait. The problem now was how
to get out on the road.

In a garage down the road from the Tent there were some
Turks who were looking for drivers. They were the agents for
Persian car importers who were trying to evade the Persian
regulations under which no citizen could bring in more than
one car a year. A Mercedes could be sold at such a profit that
it was worth the importers' while to pay westerners to drive
the car to the Persian border and then import it for them into
Persia. The importers then said that they would either pay the
import duty or arrange to have the passports stamped 'duty
paid'. This was where the trouble arose. Because once they
had got the car into Teheran the Persians tended to lose interest in this matter of one's passport. Rat had heard too much
about the problems associated with the Persian car importers,
and he was not keen on getting in touch with the garage men
down the road.

Then there was the Persian playboy who hung around the
Tent offering to take anyone who wanted to go as far as
Meshed in his Mustang. This was right across Turkey *and*
Persia, and Rat would have accepted his offer had it not been
accompanied by endless possibilities of delay, by the continual
assurance that one would be leaving tomorrow, or the day
after, or soon. And why was one Persian being so generous
anyway? Did he want to plant drugs and then smuggle them?
Was he a pimp for a Saudi male harem? Was he looking for a
fall guy for some affair that needed a fall guy? The husk of
suspicion that was to grow around Rat like armour plating
was just beginning to form. Later it led to his refusing some
of the best rides he was offered, but he hoped that it might
save him from ending up in a ditch. Rat left the playboy to
find some other fall guy.

That night it was raining hard and the travellers did not
hurry along up to the roof in their usual fashion. Instead they

lingered in the lobby and chattered and bought each other coffee and learned how to play anagrams. Bombay Pingo was teaching them how to play this game. Bombay Pingo (no one, it was generally agreed, should have a name like that) was hitching his way home to India from Cambridge, and the company deferred to his scholarship. He was teaching anagrams so well that his pupils would not leave, and the proprietor was unable to seat his regular friends in their accustomed place for coffee; so there was a fight.

During the game one of the Turks, who was watching and who had become very drunk, decided that he wanted to buy the Rat's shoes. But Rat had spent the past few days working over these shoes with a view to walking in them to India, so he was not very attracted by the Turk's proposition. To the Rat these shoes were an essential part of his professional equipment. The fact that they were strapped to his feet marked the difference between him and Bob who was in the local hospital with two broken legs after the lorry carrying him into Istanbul had crashed. Bob would be there for several months. A little note he had sent was pinned about Rat's head. 'Please come and visit me – and bring me some trousers,' it said. So long as Rat's shoes remained dry and sound he was in business as a long distance bum; he would sooner lose his pants than his shoes.

The Turk did not take his refusal at all well. All he saw was a bum wearing a curious pair of shoes which had taken his fancy and which the bum was perversely refusing to sell, even for the inflated price which the Turk was offering. Did he not trust a Turk? Was he mocking a Turk's generosity? Why did he sit there and laugh among his friends to the face of a Turk? It was an insult beyond bearing and the Turk came across to avenge himself.

Rat was puzzled by this aggression. Some drunken Turk seemed to think that he could just buy any pair of shoes and walk off in them, there and then. Who did this Turk think he was? The proprietor separated the two, and the game of anagrams continued. 'I wonder,' said Bombay Pingo, wild and unwashed and with holes in his clothes, musing over *The Times* personal column, 'I wonder what would happen if someone put in one of these ads "Wanted, holiday companion for Majorca" and I turned up?' The group looked at him. It would have been an unusual interview.

And suddenly, no one was quite sure how, no one quite knew why, it was agreed by about twenty of the group that on the very next morning they would leave. They were tired of the Tent, and Istanbul and the tourists. They were frightened by the police force and they wanted regular supplies of cannabis. The money was running out and the town was a drag, and they were ready to go. They were heading out there, east, beyond police forces, where the sun came from ... to Katmandu.

And when they had announced this and gone up to the Tent to sleep and left the lobby empty, Rat looked around and thought a bit and wondered if he might go too. It was partly big Louis and his long knife, it was partly Thor and the Clown, it was partly the police; something of all these persuaded Rat to leave, but it was mainly his private restlessness.

If he was not going to drive a Persian Mercedes, and he was not going to be driven in a Persian Mustang, it seemed to Rat that there was only one thing left: he would have to hitch. And he would start the very next morning.

Just before he left, the old Yugoslav woman who cleaned out the rooms came to speak to him. She wore a faded blue dress and black wool stockings, and her Christian status in this heathen country was somehow proclaimed by the thick, white scarf which covered her hair. She said that she too was a traveller – she had been to Greece and Italy and since her youth had worked here in Turkey. Most of all she wanted to return home to Yugoslavia, everybody wanted to return home in the end. She was lonely, but she did not suppose that she would ever leave Turkey now. Was Rat lonely? Yes, doubtless Rat was lonely. Did he have a signorina? For five lire she would be his signorina.

But Rat walked out of the Gulhane that morning, and so he had to leave without his signorina. He walked down the hill, away from the Blue Mosque, past the hot bread shop and into the maze of street markets. It was raining gently, a Kerry rain, fine soft weather. Grumbling about the unaccustomed weight of his pack, he made his way out of the other side of the markets and down to the water side. He passed the shabby railway station, the terminus of the Orient Express, with the faded red and gold paint on its wooden canopy, and the crowds of spivs who hung round the taxi queues at the entrance.

On the quays the clubs were advertising the 'Dr Barnard Strip', rumours about the details of which were in the best traditions of the capital of the Levant, and other posters advertised 'Arcelik', which disappointingly had turned out to be a Turkish refrigerator. The whole town seemed a botch job that morning. Perched on the edge of Asia, the last outpost of the west, it was a place on the road to somewhere else, a good place to be leaving. Rat could bear the stares and the laughter and the pig-ignorance of the bystanders now ... He was back on the road. Nobody minded a town laughing at you if you were walking out of it. Look, Rat could say, I rejected you first. You are so ugly that I prefer even the open road to you.

Past the quays where the fat ships from Greece and Russia unloaded, over the long and steeply pitched bridge to the other side of the Golden Horn, and the minor boat to Asia Minor. He carried the weight on his back proudly now, he bent to it, fitting the uneven surfaces together, bearing his own load. Descending from the crest of the bridge on to the far shore he gathered speed and the crowd made sure to jump out of his way. The rain had stopped, the gulls wheeled in the moist air, the boat sirens sounded out; somewhere on the hill behind came the nasal cry of an amplified muezzin.

His back was to all that. He was going on a journey, in time and in wisdom, and over six lands he had never seen before. He had to submit himself, like a novice to the Rule, to the disciplines and demands of this achievement. He was a man who had forgotten who he was. He knew his name, he remembered the minute details of his days, but he no longer knew where the world ended, and he began. As a boy he had been *there*, he had been *him*, and outside there had been the rest, the other, the not him. He could no longer draw this line, the division had been obscured by so many other views on the matter. To resolve this uncertainty he was setting out in search of that boy, and in search of that life which he had once known was waiting.

Rat was running now, running down the bridge, running along the quay and on to the boat. He was running into a strange landscape, from an unfamiliar fear, to an uncertain haven. Running was how we first saw Rat.

II Two toads and a rat

It was night time. From the high bench at the back of the lorry's cab John Perkins and I could sit and watch our crew, in the glow of the panel-light, bend to their tasks. There was room for all on that bench, even though John Perkins, my companion, was a man who bore many cameras. These he concealed in cloth bags and about his person, but skilfully and so as not to incommode him. A strong man Perkins, and one occasionally visited by the divine gift of silence. On the high bench we could talk and speculate and doze and disagree, all at will and in no order, comforted by the sense of having left a place that morning where men rose and worked and ate and slept, as they had done yesterday and would do tomorrow; all by routine and without perception and with no eye for the many possibilities of the moment. Sometimes our team lit thick-smelling cigarettes, sometimes they muttered a conversation, sometimes they shifted in their seats, always they stared ahead; and so we thundered on through that first night.

Once or twice there came an interruption. A lorry in front, a slower model naturally, might be offering a more than conventional resistance to being overtaken. A special effort was called for, a virtuoso display of harrying tactics. We overtook the lorry, we let him draw ahead. We doubled him again. Our driver pulled into the middle of the road and began to slow down. We paused on a hill, the lorry behind struggling to keep going. He flashed his lights and our commander stood on his pedals and leant out of his window and stared wordlessly back. All this time we rushed on up the slope. Attila had one outstretched foot on the accelerator, one arm on the great wheel. His assistant, charged with the importance of his task, kept his eyes on the road and sounded the horn and operated the direction indicators in spectacular sequence. For half a minute this continued. Our man standing out of his window staring steadily back, lit by the glare of his opponent's lights, a cigarette in his mouth, not a sound coming out of it. Still looking back he changed gear and then returned to his seat. As a demonstration of willpower it was certainly effective. We heard no more from the creature behind. The team redoubled their efforts, paying an excessive attention to the tiny details of movement involved in operating an indicator or sounding the horn or wiping the glass. Such preoccupation demanded a cargo of nitro-glycerine at least.

Towards midnight they dropped us at the petrol station which terminated their journey. It was beside the main road but well away from any village. There was a cafe, and we decided to eat and then to spend the night, which was now dry, beside the road. Outside the lorries picked each other out again and again. We could afford to ignore them for some hours now, we had that much confidence in the future of our journey.

It had started on the ferry with Captain Anatoli Pekmen, the noted Expert and Official Lecturer on Classical Istanbul. Captain Pekmen had been sitting on the bench outside the ferry's saloon keeping abreast of events by reading the airmail edition of *The Times*. It was raining, and the airmail edition had been getting a little flimsier with each movement. Captain Pekmen had persevered until he had finished, and then he had introduced himself.

He was, it transpired, the man who had shown Winston Churchill round Istanbul. He was, even now, the captain of a ketch, and he was, still more to the point, the man who had something up his sleeve for *us*. Somebody we should meet, just round the corner here. It was the wild figure we had first seen running down the bridge. It was Rat. He joined us. And Captain Pekmen, having effected this introduction and enquired our destination – announced that he would put us on our way. He directed us to the Florence Nightingale Hospital, and to the Florence Nightingale Cemetery, and to the bus which would take us out to the highway; and so misled by the great navigator we made our way happily towards the Black Sea instead of Ankara. Pointed towards Ankara and Incili and Karasu, we eventually descended from the bus and checked our direction with some road menders. The road menders had played this game before.

Bus drops purposeful looking Europeans carrying large bags who ask the way to Iran. Who can divine such mysteries as the way to Iran? But the foreigners must be humoured. Send them to Ankara which all the world knows is east, send them back to Stamboul which is west, send them anywhere for they are piggishly stupid and have no sensible conversation at all. An old diesel taxi, a *dolmus*, took us back to our proper point of departure. Agva and Incili and Karasu were relinquished when the taste of them had only begun to sweeten our journey. Instead we sat by the side of a brand new road, under a high bank of gravel and waited for our first ride. It was raining lightly but that was of no importance.

After some minutes in the drizzle a small Desoto truck drew up and Grigoire, an Armenian too happy to be fully in the possession of his faculties, tossed our bags into the back and hauled us up into the stenchy comfort of the cabins. If you try to hitch in the west when it is raining you soon get so wet that no one wants you in his car. Grigoire had a different approach. If he offered a ride when it was raining he offered the full treatment. You all got damp together, you all thawed out together. He had a remarkable scraggy beard, many gold teeth and a high-pitched cackle which he rattled round the cabin when John made train noises on his harmonica. He shared his oranges. He was a kind man, and not a bit talkative.

Asia, like Europe, was flat and sparse. The first water buffalo should have been an exotic touch but the creature looked disappointingly like a cow. We passed no other travellers. It had not occurred to us that we might go from Istanbul to Katmandu and scarcely pass another traveller. Grigoire drove us into the middle of the afternoon and set us down by a garage. Then he disappeared down a little road to the south with a wave and a cackle. We missed him.

The garage stood below the main road, and beside it was a hovel with a fridge, where one could buy meat and bread and yogurt. We took turns standing guard on the road and going down to eat. Two little boys from their vantage point on the rising ground opposite amused themselves with wild mockery of our signals and by throwing the occasional flint. Quite deliberately they aimed for vulnerable parts. All the time they were watched by an indulgent old man. If we shouted or moved towards them they ran as though for their lives and the old man scowled. They were playing fair game.

After an hour or so a commercial gentleman in a Chevrolet bore us off from their tormentings and expressed the hope that their balls might wither. He was another kind man but he spoke good English and he talked too much about textiles and tyre factories. We were passing through a good area for tyre factories. In Duzce, in the dusk, he left us. It was still raining and there was little traffic. Another lift seemed unlikely. Every time we tried to signal a lorry a crowd of children mimicked our actions and hid us from sight. We were mobbed like owls who had ventured out too early, and we could not twist them off. Walking in the mud by the road we stumbled over Sam from Islington. He had taken two days to get this far, and was waiting for the children to grow bored of their game. He and his mate Pete were on their way to Kuwait, but Pete, trying to make better progress, had gone ahead alone. Sam gave the mob a diversion. Sitting in the mud he was a stricken owl, and more tempting, and once we were clear of him we attracted the attention of a Shell tanker.

The last we saw of Sam he was still surrounded and still sitting down. We felt no regret at abandoning him. The tanker was already crowded. No question of anyone giving up his place for Sam. Chance had united us, chance had divided us; chance would unite us again just as soon as he got on his feet and found a ride of his own. Travelling, we were one of a privileged company, part of the pursuit. To join in, all you needed was a ride. Without a ride you were not so much a person as a place. And, as Rat said, you had to be quite a big place before the rest of us would climb off the train and pay a call. Places were what we were travelling from. Sam was just a heap by the road place, and we left him.

This new driver, the Overtaker, was a man of some skill, and the possessor of a fully qualified assistant, a younger and a scrubbier man, an apprentice to the trade of lorry driving. Quite soon after we boarded it the tanker pulled up outside a mud-spattered cafe and our commander disappeared to transact a little business upstairs. His mate produced a tool kit and a heavy wooden mallet with which he bashed a selection of the many wheels. Sometimes he bashed one of the watching crowd of children instead. These children were much better brought up than the others. They made a point of returning the mallet if he flung it at them, and when we climbed down they gathered round to offer us bread and to refuse our lemonade, and they queued up to brush down our baggage.

While they were at this the mate was working feverishly at one unnecessary task after another. His object was to prove that his was the most important lorry in the park, and that, by extension, he was the most important assistant lorry driver. The striking of a match within throwing distance of the tanker would drive him frantic. The vehicle was ringed with discarded tools. It was only a medium-to-small Shell tanker, but his imaginary tasks were charged with urgency and his energy was rewarded by a large crowd. When the driver reappeared he became frantic again in striving to gather everything in time. He certainly could pack a tool kit quickly. The driver climbed in and started up without so much as looking at him. We all scrambled aboard. As we pulled out the mate was hanging on to the front, kneeling on the bonnet furiously polishing the windscreen. The driver waved him impatiently inside. Immediately he leapt for the door, and sat there tensed, waiting for the next muttered instructions. The more active and willing he became the more sullen grew his chief. For the driver it was a species of humiliation. He did not feel comfortable while his assistant played slave-boy. The flamboyant self-abasement exaggerated, and therefore threw into question, his own position as commander. We enjoyed every moment of their performance, and accepted their cigarettes, and called them our boys.

As it happened we did not have to spend that first night in the open. When we had finished our meal, someone from the next table asked us where we were going. He was Halim, the owner of the garage and of the cafe, and he was a student at Ankara University. He told us that we could spend the night on the floor of one of his sheds and that in the morning, at dawn, he would take us the rest of the way to Ankara. The evening was spent in the garage, drinking and playing cards. Halim remembered other travellers who had passed this way. One had tried to pass on the far side of the road. The men had offered him food and a lift but he had been too frightened to accept. He had run from them and from their friendliness; why? Rat thought that he had probably stolen something.

The mechanics at that garage were very great smokers. They sold us hash, and we sold them packets of duty-free State Express. These were a considerable status symbol, the bidding was high, and we finished the day on a dry concrete floor with far more money than we had started it. We slept behind a long plate-glass window. And those who passed that night would have seen three of their number momentarily lit in the headlights, dozing in their bags like fish in the bottom of an aquarium. Publicly resting, and on their way.

Halim kept his word and returned at dawn. We left the boys sleeping in a shed behind the petrol pumps, six of them on the one broad bench, huddled together like hounds, clutching their State Express. They had been working the pumps all night. We reached Ankara quickly enough. The land had changed in the hills we had passed over the night before. It was richer, forests and wheat fields and orchards and summer grazing. Sometimes we passed a deserted wooden village where whole communities would come to live with their herds during the summer. Ankara was dry and windy. On every street corner industrious sweepers stirred up the dust into the gusty air. It was a city with a provincial air, unlike Istanbul, and there was a stillness about it as though it was waiting, if not for one of its periodic earthquakes then for the traditional violence of the coming elections. 'A few hundred people were usually killed in election week', we were told. Halim drove us right across, and it was a relief to regain the country on the far side. He dropped us at a large cross roads and wished us luck. The Rat promised to write from Katmandu. Halim's last words were a warning.

'Go by the coast road, go down to the sea. Don't go through the centre.' Why not? 'There are tribes there, not Kurds but like Kurds. They are not good people. Go by the sea.'

We thanked him and promised to follow his advice, and we knew that we would not bother with it at all. The sea was to the north and we were heading east. 'Tribes like Kurds' sounded just right.

It was a sunny, blustery day. We set off up a hill, a long straight empty road, and our first whole day. A soldier in a Morris Minor stopped and somehow we loaded ourselves into the back seat. Beside him, in the front seat, his girl friend, massive and merry, bounced from bump to bump. To begin with he indicated that he would take us the 650 miles to Erzerum near the Persian border, the last town in Turkey, but in the event he dropped us after a few hundred yards outside his camp. It took us as long a time to struggle out of the car, looking back down the hill we could see the point at which we had struggled in.

Walking down the hill to Persia amid the schoolchildren, dressed in their black Mao smocks, walking down the hill to their lunch and showing us their homework; crossing a river where the broad new road became a lane, hitching a ride in the back of a Skoda truck, sitting in the sunshine in the wind at the back, the wind so loud that we could not hear our own singing, hot in the sun and cooled in the wind, swept in and out of unpaved villages, across a blue-green empty field country, nothing moving but the grass and the trees, and those bucking and pitching all day, whistling into the wind, racing a great black steam train that howled from hill to hill, bounding between the distances, tearing up the shallow hills and down the dusty roads, poop, poop, travellers like Toad, like Toad surrounded by other people's horizons.

Luncheon was taken at Kirikkale; and the tourist toads in the back of the light-blue Skoda were feted. How many 'toorestes' had Kirikkale seen before? We drove from house to house waving regally, receiving flowers and tea, and distributing generously the compliment of our full attention. We took yogurt with our hosts and as we prepared to depart a great crowd of admirers gathered. Roses were exchanged, the town barber demanded, and was granted, a close-up examination, photographs were bestowed. They tried to pinch an arm, they tried to pinch a map – how could they adequately mark our departure, adequately to match the warmth of their welcome? As we drove away the smallest boy spat, bullseye in my ear. 'Goal, Goal!' The assembly rose to its feet, the departure was very adequately marked, the toads, the toorestes, were sped.

It rained on us in the afternoon, so we climbed into our sleeping bags and opened out our groundsheet and lay on the floor of the truck and became hysterical at the superfluity of our arrangements. An impossible journey, a demented plan, to cross overland to India without any transport, and now bounding towards Persia at 50 m.p.h. in a truck big enough for six, in sleeping bags thick enough for the Arctic, carrying supplies enough for an army, through a country beautiful enough to compass the rest of our lives. So much excess evoked several miles of hysterical laughter, calmed only by the addition of another passenger, a taciturn peasant of the region in a wide flat hat and dark suit, with stained yellow fingers. He crossed his legs at the back of the truck and stared and stared and smelled of saffron. The rain stopped and we climbed on to a drabber plain with meaner houses. The Rat remarked that at times it was hard to tell whether they were inhabited by men or their beasts. With a bump we stopped at Yozgat, sixty miles down the road through the centre of the country. We thanked our driver who was going no further and prepared to depart, and he mentioned that we owed him rather a lot of money.

Inflamed by a bad day's carrying and by a sight of the money we had used in Kirikkale our driver had turned 'auto-stop' into a bus ride. He wanted five pounds.

No.

This was only petrol money since he had come all the way from Ankara solely on our account.

No.

His mate, an honest man with a squint and a few words of the French, translated unhappily. He was prepared to agree privately that it had been 'autostop'. We decided that the only thing to do was to abandon the exchange and leave the town. We started to walk away, neither of them followed us, and we were left with the children who had gathered in unusual numbers at the sight of the freaky argument. We made our way out towards the edge of town and talked to them. For some reason in Yozgat the school taught English rather than French or German and they had many words to test out. As we reached the outskirts there was a shout behind. The carrier was back with a policeman.

Act stupid, go limp, smile and walk on. The policeman unbuttoned his holster. Smile and walk back. Rat had it all off pat.

Our child interpreters became very pessimistic. 'He bad poleece. Make you sleep at poleece house. Are you angree? I veree sorry'. We were not angry. If they arrested us, they arrested us.

The police house was a rotten shed smelling, let us be frank, of shit. Inside was a horrible sight. The chief officer was the very same Bey who had had such fun with lily-white Lawrence in the film. All lies about the Bey being an actor. He was still a Bey, and he crouched in a police house in Yozgat and trapped unwary Englishmen just like the old days in Jordan. The English class were left at the doors, but two star

pupils were allowed in to interpret. They were between eight
and nine. At first our side worked well together. The driver
stated his complaint and was savagely abused by the Bey –
who seemed to be in uncommonly bad temper. So long as he
was not up to his old desert tricks, so long as he was not lust-
ing after any caucasian flesh, we might get away with it. The
phrase 'autostop' was repeated again and again. Our team
jumped up and down just as though they were back in Kirikkale – 'ees good, vair good'. How to restrain their enthusiasm
tactfully, lest they be ejected and we have to fight without
words? Surely even the Bey would not carry out a nipple
inspection in front of the village infant class? He was looking
thoughtful, he was fingering his typewriter ... The door burst
open. It was the second officer, a man far too repulsive to be
involved in any subtleties. Were we saved? The children
were thrown out bodily, the carrier was thrown out bodily. It
was our turn. An argument broke out between the Bey and
the Second. The Bey lost and resumed typing. The Second
demanded our passports.

We spent an hour in there copying out our passports.
Finally Rat got us out. He knew all about policemen. He did
as he was told, he smiled, he knew when not to correct the
Second's spelling, he *accommodated* him. We kept as far from
his grossness as possible, Rat *contained* it. We got out of there.
When the details were all done, the Second decided that an
impressive exit was in order. He shouted, he ranted, he worked
himself into a rage. He was drawing his dirty boot back, he
was grabbing for the nearest bag, and we fell down the stairs
and into the street and amongst our football team.

'Rad, Jan. Ees good.' Was good.

And that Second was so 'angree' that he missed an opportunity to get one of us five years in jail. For somewhere at the
bottom of one of our sacks was the little silver foil package we
had purchased at Halim's garage.

Now blinking in the sunshine surrounded by the dancing boys outside the rank police house we could laugh. Once again we were escorted to the edge of Yozgat. They set us on the road to Sivas, 'goodbyee, goodbyee', anxious and good-humoured and solicitous and bilingual. We hoped they would never become second officers. It was early evening and the rain clouds were threatening to fill the mud holes of the town. Somewhere in one of the bars an inflamed and thwarted carrier was brooding on his failed gyp. We did not want to linger in Yozgat. The beauty of that day had deceived us. It was very much of the West to be arrested and questioned and inspected and filed away. It was very much of the West to argue over a non-existent fare. As we travelled, the West seemed to travel with us. We shifted direction together. But there was nothing visible on the hills beyond the village, no definite phantoms were in pursuit. The first car that passed stopped: a plush saloon that drove on and then reversed. It carried a father and son, the latter of an age with our interpreters and equally anxious to practise his English. And so we travelled away from that shadow behind the hills, but we carried with us, in the child's shy questions, an echo of its voice.

That evening after passing through pine woods to where the road ran for some miles beside a stream we saw a flooded house. It stood quite alone surrounded by great trees and a small lake, and an old lady, its owner, stood at her doorway in the dusk looking out at her friends on the road, who sometimes called to her. She peered at them through the gloom and said nothing. A little further down the road the stream had swollen into a torrent and burst across our path. On each side there was a queue of lorries and buses, and men in flat hats and black coats, with their striped trousers rolled up to their knees, gingerly tested the depth. It was just narrow enough to shout across. In the centre of the torrent two lorries had been over-turned. They lay on their sides, like beasts which have been shot at full gallop, and one of them had spilled bricks into the stream. There was talk now of trying again and it seemed sensible that one of the high-axled lorries or an empty bus should lead the way, but those lorry drivers had a commercial interest in their journeys, and as they looked at the wrecks in front of them they seemed to hesitate.

Unable to justify the contrast between their eagerness to see the road opened and their reluctance to be the ones to do it, the lorry drivers lost face and were brushed aside. But our driver was a prosperous man with a glittering saloon and a position to maintain before his small son and the strangers who rode with him. A muscular man with clear eyes and hairy forearms, a man with a system who believed in technique. Time to apply some. He hurried us back into his car, bustled his way to the head of the queue and plunged in. The car lurched as he accelerated and we looked suspiciously at the water level rising to the bottom of the door. We hit a hole and some stones and slewed in the middle of the stream beneath the tall sides of the overturned lorries. To our right the water rippled over the edge of the submerged road. Somehow, and with the enthusiastic encouragement of the watchers, we reached the other shore. Tremendous applause all round, in which we joined. The water had started to rise again and we were the only car to cross that night. We tore on through the night, over a worsening road, to Sivas.

Whether he was going further or not our driver put us off in Sivas. We had made 300 miles that day. We found some rooms and had supper in a cafe with four Turkish boys who were enjoying their last meal before starting two years of military service. They were from Istanbul and spoke good French. A Jewish musician, a Jewish pharmacist, an Armenian barber and a Greek jam manufacturer, all melancholy at the thought of the time ahead in Turkey's enormous army, all mourning Istanbul, to which they kissed their hands. Their heads were already shaven in preparation for the lice of their service, and they had a disturbing resemblance to each other, each a living skull with enormous eyes and gaunt cheeks, like military monks. When we stopped talking and they had heard of where we were going they fell silent, thinking about our journey and their confinement. Our travels magnified their restrictions and they grew restless with their diminished world. They were resentful of the inequality, and the jam manufacturer allowed himself a few maudlin tears before carrying the little pharmacist to bed. The harmonica was produced and we adjourned to their room where they were soon spiritedly weeping away to the blues. The owner of the rooms arrived with a number of complaints and rescued us from the pool of tears. When we rose in the morning they had already left for camp.

Lying awake that night thinking of the day's progress, listening to the few noises of the quietening town, it seemed possible to estimate the exact future length of our journey. 300 miles a day would bring us to Persia in two days, to Afghanistan in a week and to India within three. A month on the road did not seem long enough. Such was our enthusiasm for this journey that we felt that we ought to slow our rush, a late start in the morning seemed appropriate. Two days on the road and already we felt able to arrange a more reflective pace. Sleep came to the sound of harness bells outside the window. The point where the river had burst its banks was on a latitude with Jerusalem and marked the farthest point east in the Rat's life. He should have made something out of that, a river springing up to block his path on the latitude of Jerusalem as he moved beyond his extant world. It was a portent, and he should have polished it.

We slept well in Sivas. Separated from the disasters and pleasure of tomorrow by the night, one of the great nights which towered up on that journey and distinguished the passage of events, strange nights in a strange country, tumbling out of the chaotic hours that passed in regions where we had no bearings in time or space, we slept well. They were familiar abysses in which we could find refuge from the sequence of haphazard patterns that we followed. On the road we lingered in our nights.

Next morning, as we promised, we rose late and took a stately breakfast in the dark kitchen at the back of the cafe. A dozen women in thick scarves were preparing vegetables and rice and some scrawny meat. Hens ran between the benches and one was scooped up and made ready for the day's kebab. Even in this room, the men were in charge. Occasionally the chef stirred something that smelled nice while all the work was done by their mothers and grand-mothers and sisters; and all the orders came from the pro-prietor, lounging sleekly in the front room and entertaining some of his friends to a game of cards and a glass of tea. Turkey is a Moslem country, and while the men are allowed authority over the family, the women are meant to have authority in the household; but the news has yet to reach the kitchens of Sivas.

Towards midday we hitched up our bags, which, despite the confident assertions of those just off the road in Istanbul, were not growing any lighter, and set off down the length of the main street. Past the vegetable shops, with their fluorescent wares, bright reds and yellows and deep blues, all the colours vegetables are not, and past the jingling horse carriages. The town fire brigade came roaring up the muddy highway in fine style, the bell ringing and the firemen hanging out in a quite unnecessary way. The engine thundered past at eight miles an hour, red paint and great brass bells and comic opera uniforms – a prized exhibit in any other country's transport museum. Walking down the high street towards the east it was difficult to see the way out of town. There was only a cart track which wound up through some trees to the plain above.

As we picked our way through the mud, accompanied by the children on their way to lunch, we noticed a crowd gathered outside the door of a shop. This was unusual and our professional pride was piqued. We had already become accustomed to the attention we attracted everywhere, and were now jealous that in Sivas there should be some sight to distract those who normally devoted their curiosity to us. Mobs had become a tribute to our rarity, they reassured us of our existence, and we played to them as to a gallery. For all we knew, the next village, the next mob, might be several hours away, we wanted to make the most of the present one.

Rat walked over to the door and peered through the tightly pressed bodies. Then he beckoned us back and reluctantly we retraced our steps into the street. The crowd was gathered outside a cafe and after a while, between the slabs of rotting meat set to soften in the sun, we could make out an unusual sight for that country: four bronzed thighs, two short-trousered travellers, the first we had seen since Sam from Islington on the far side of Ankara. When they had finished their meal we ascended the cart track together, in a celebration of massed mobs. One of the newcomers was a girl, and in her sawn-off jeans she proved sufficient curiosity for the children to accompany us all the way up the hill and out of the village.

'Erzincan?' they asked.

'Erzincan.'

'Erzerum?'

'Yes. Erzincan, Erzerum,' we replied.

'Erzincan. Erzerum....?' they shouted, and waited for the next place on our list. The names on the road ahead clanged between us. Kars, Erivan, Agri, names that must have been first spoken by the crows, Erivan and Erzerum and Erzincan. Were they related to the city called Er? Ur of the Chaldees. The children did not bother with such metaphysics and the Rat composed a chant to satisfy them.

'Erzerum, Iran, Afghanistan, Pakistan, Hindustan (an inspiration this), Nepal'. Nepal brought blank looks. 'Katmandu'. It meant nothing. And anyway why had we stopped? Where next? At the top of the hill the track dried out and we could look back on to Sivas, ringed by its trees and fields. As their town dropped out of sight the children began to turn back, they would not go beyond sight of their homes. Once or twice the wind brought us the litany from their retreating forms – 'Iran-afghanis-tanpakis-tanhindus-tankatmand-duna-poli'.

Ahead was a great level plain with broken grassland and cornfields on each side. We were walking along the raised spine of a plateau, with the land sloping gradually away from us to the plain's edge and the blue sky beneath our feet bordering either horizon. A sunny day, no wind, walking on the outside of the world. Hot. A haze. A red bird like a magpie chattered on the wire which ran beside the road into the un-sighted distance. The bird was a solitary token of life ahead; the only hint that we were not the first to reach this place. It preceded our steps, fluttering on and on down the wire into the haze, where it shimmered and beckoned. We trudged clumsily, silently, after it. Behind us came – no one. No one followed us up the hill. Quite possibly it was a question of walking from here through this haze to India. The heat's crowded silence boomed around us.

For an hour or two we walked along the road content. Once we passed some gypsies camped a few hundred yards below the road. They looked at us and we stared back at their yapping dogs and veiled women, hard to say which of us the more suspicious. With their black tents they resembled desert

Bedouin. The dogs made a token pass in our direction, the women went inside the tent. One of the men watched warily. The tents took on the air of a besieged community, crouched beneath a skyline along which tramped the temporarily nomadic armies of the West. One grandfather emerged and bawled and waved and made smoking gestures. The fame of the leaf had preceded us.

Further along the ridge an enormous jagged figure swayed out of the mist. At about fifty yards it sprang apart and into focus and became two women carrying water to the gypsies. Two gypsy women who scurried by on the edge of the narrow track, pulling their shawls around their faces, and never once glancing back beneath their load. Their fear chilled us in the afternoon's heat.

After a while we began to tire of dragging our packs and to look anxiously back. There had been no side tracks so we had not missed the way. A tiny donkey cart approached and we rested. An old man was driving, slowly, and two veiled women squatted in the back. They were all tiny, but the cart seemed about to collapse under their weight, and the donkey, like his driver, was old and slow. We considered clambering aboard, but let it pass, which was as well. When we resumed walking we found we were catching up on it.

Later two farm carts loomed up. The first was crowded with labourers and drawn by a powerful tractor. It ignored our signals. The second approached and we tried again. It contained the labourers' wives, clustered together, their dark eyes staring back. 'Never bother with the second cart,' said Barry.

His appearance was deceptive, tanned and fresh, with his jeans cut off above the knee since a sunny day in Bulgaria. It had been the first sunny day, and they were going south, and it would never rain again. It had rained steadily ever since. He had travelled this road before, by himself, some years earlier. Then he had worn the hair, and smuggled hash, and been mistaken for Jesus Christ by a moslem fanatic in a Persian bazaar. When the mistake was discovered he was pelted with stones. Barry had a dry recollection of this incident – 'it made a change from "get your hair cut".'

Now he was a reformed character, hitching to Australia with his girl, whose home was there. He never expected to return to England, and this route provided him with a proper farewell to the north. Overland to Madras, and then by boat and road to Singapore and Darwin. Ann was a self-contained person with a devastating ability to unman the natives if they got a little out of hand. Like Maud's brother, she simply gorgonised them from head to foot with a stony British stare. She was one of the few girls we met on the road. Not many travellers wanted to expend that much energy in guarding them. In Istanbul, rape stories had been exchanged like football scores.

Barry had no such problems. Instead in his slow progress down the world, marked by a trail of petrified lechers, like pillars by the wayside, he savoured the advantages of his lack of speed, and the period of time gained between two jobs as a draughtsman. A time when he could gather a proper appreciation of the distances and peoples and circumstances linked by his journey. He bore in his mind's map an indistinguishable impression of distance covered, and of time passed. His days were founded on the memory of the countless earlier journeys, over the land and through the climates, which he was repeating. He seemed unable to slough off this accreted mental impression.

'If,' he asked, 'you fly from London to Sydney in thirty-six hours, a journey which has always taken as many weeks, and you feel sick when you arrive, is it surprising?' He began to explain his theory that if more Australians had travelled to their country overland, they would never have adopted a white Australia policy. An unlikely weapon with which to combat

Wasp racialism, forged on a sunny afternoon, on a windy road, in the east of Anatolia.

At about four-thirty that afternoon the third vehicle of the day came along. It was a bus and we surrendered on sight. Some brisk bargaining with the driver established that he would do us a special party rate to Zara. Forty miles for ten lire the lot. As we climbed aboard we told each other despairingly that we had not left Istanbul to take bus rides. We were the *pic-assiettes* of this road, living off our wits, our journey constituting a total rejection of the philosophy of international money and the world of timetables. Yesterday had we not risked arrest, ridicule, even delay, to emphasise this principle? Had we not gypped a common carrier (a man without influence or resources) out of his rightfully earned pittance? And now, here we were in an autobus, a charabanc, for all the world like some seaside mystery tour, being carried solely on the sufferance of our fares and at the mercy of an officious conductor. Life was hard.

Zara was a town a third the size of Sivas. Where the ridge ended the bus stopped and the sun went in. It was here that the road took a jagged fork north to reach a pass through the mountains guarding the east. That morning's rutted track had been described on the map as 'a loose-surfaced road of good standard'. Ahead the map said there was 'a loose-surfaced road of low standard'. Over the pass. It was getting colder, we had covered barely forty miles. That was not a day's journey. As we walked out of the village a gang of stocky men joined the children. They were anxious for Ann to stay, and they could not be persuaded to unblock the path until a passing patriarch had abused them. We thanked him.

Down a narrow avenue of tall poplars, and just as the first hills began to close on the road, the first car of the day approached and stopped. It seemed too small for everyone, and we began to regret joining forces. Two of us, on that chill evening, would have to wait by the road. But the driver would have none of it. Somehow he managed to load us up, and we moved off in the warmth of mutual regard, us for his kindness, he for our gratitude. And so were carried over the mountains into the lushness of the central plains.

As we climbed it became bitterly cold outside, and we were glad to be huddled in the warmth of his saloon rather than the back of a farm truck. The air was clear and hard, there was snow on the road, we were surely passing through a country of wolves and bears. Once we had to leave the car to push it through a stream, round a lorry that had jack-knifed across the track, an incident that seemed suitable on a road built for stage coaches. At the head of the pass there was a tablet set into the rock wall by the road, commemorating the nine-teenth-century engineer who had made it. The tablet dated the achievement. Just here the track was narrow and pitted, with ice forming in the streams which frequently crossed it. It was not a moment to tell our host that little seemed to have been done since the road was built, but Rat did tell him so.

Towards dusk we dropped down on the far side of the range. The mountains' crests around were afire, and the mur-murs from the herds below, and the smoke from the farms, rose straight in the evening air. 'Well Come,' said a sign at the entrance to the village. 'Well Come to Susehri.'

The commercial traveller who had brought us over the mountains was staying here overnight and then returning to Sivas so we would have to find another way out of the village. We left him and looked around the square. As we passed down the row of wooden houses we noticed one of the big trucks which we had left on the far side of the flooded river on the evening before. It was a multicoloured Mercedes with a brass lion's face on the radiator grill, the same raucous crew beside it, and still loaded far too high with something which swelled the tarpaulins and dripped steadily into the dust.

Surely that lion's face implied a Persian lorry, on its way to the border? The cargo dripped away. The truck hinted at magical properties; it had not passed us on the road, it could not have come the way we had come over that pass, but here it was, dripping impatiently to be gone east. There seemed room for all in its vast cab. Then there was a stir in the crowd that had gathered silently around us. Sayin Seyfettin Simsek had arrived.

Sayin Seyfettin Simsek was a man on the verge of his life's work. By day he was a bank clerk, and, as he immediately assured us, he only mentioned this in case we wanted him to open the bank right *now*, this minute. Was there anything at all that we needed? For one thing it seemed clear to him that we needed a cup of tea and he would provide that at once. He was young and slight, he wore his overcoat round his shoulders, and he led us lightly over to a house where tea was served as soon as we had sat down. We did not pay for this, it was served at the expense of Susehri. If he ordered tea for some strangers it came without argument, for was he not also the commissar of the local tourist board, and just now making a fairly serious error about the nature of these new arrivals, and the immediate allocation of the bureau's funds? Could he not hear the distant tramp of approaching armies, laden with travellers' cheques? And had it not become a simple matter of diverting a few of them into the local hostelries? Free tea then while Sayin spoke with the toorestes.

Did we like his 'Well Come' notice, was it not splendid, would we care to cast our eyes over his B.B.C. language course, just to reassure ourselves that he was versed in all the official rites? See the blue label on the envelope, toorestes? Official, B.B.C. He was poised by his Rubicon, this Simsek. Let his fellow peasants but cooperate for a few months and the legend of Susehri would loom large in the lives of men from the Andes to the Aral Sea. Or it might at least reach the ears and pockets of those who wrote the government tourist brochures. 'These are tourestes, these are my freends, drink up my freends, drink your chay,' your clear golden tea, sweet and in fragile cruets, sweet and hot and golden like mulled honey. Susehri lay beneath the mountains on the hem of Anatolia, thirsting for the presence of these strangers who had invaded the country from the west, thirsting for no matter which of them, as long as they too were thirsty and paid in good travellers' cheques. Just now the village streets were unpaved, its small houses made of painted wood, its rose gardens unfenced, its orchards open for beasts and people to wander through. For the time its inhabitants' lives were governed by the need to make things grow, their days shaped in response to the seasons, and there was a small army post at each end of the village to discourage robbers. For the time Susehri existed in the primitive conditions of England's deepest countryside in the late nineteenth century. But Sayin Seyfettin Simsek was going to change all that. There was a little gleam in his eye that told the story. He was a charming fellow, and prodigiously destructive.

'You will stay here my friends, in Susehri, the most beautiful village in Anatolia, and in Turkey. You know Susan Freeson? She lives in London. She is my pen friend. She is beautiful, I think. You will stay here in this hotel –' he pointed to the balcony above – 'I will fix.' The crowd looked pleased, Sayin was going to fix, there was a little gleam in his eye and he knew. Well of course we would stay there. We were tired, it was evening, we had crossed the mountains and the village was so peaceful. We would stay, as he kept on telling us while we looked at his collection of photographs and debated whether to open his bank up, and we all considered whether or not to correct his 'welcome' sign, about whose correctness he was very anxious. The village gathered round to inspect their old mate Sayin's latest haul, to assess whether the month's budget

for the tourist board had been well spent, to calculate the possibilities of a deal on their own account with these hairy
foreigners. Sayin worked away, keeping their curiosity satisfied, keeping up the sweet talk with us. Beyond our group, two
tatty happy soldiers wandered past hand in hand, the light
behind the chalets and orchards warmed the quiet streets, and
the lion lorry slipped down the hill out of the village. And
Sayin, suddenly sensing the unexpected restlessness in us,
which he must have put down to the departing lorry, seized
our baggage and made for the stairs.

And then we knew that we would not after all be staying
that night in Susehri. A hundred miles was not a respectable
total for five hard nuts on the road to Katmandu. Not after the
day before had brought in three hundred miles and one arrest,
not even taking the mountains into consideration, not at all
or by any account. Susehri was beautiful, but the next village
would doubtless be the same, and the sooner we were there the
better.

These were the reasons we told each other as we recovered
our cases, but they were not the real ones. The real ones were
to do with that gleam in the eye of our principal host. For who
knew when we would ever get away from Mr Simsek once we
had accepted his hospitality? How many toorestes came *down*
those steps behind him? Who knew that this village in the
fold of the mountains was not enchanted, that Mr Simsek
would not be even more pressing in his invitations on the next
day, that he would find our company so completely satisfactory that he would always be this unwilling for us to leave?
So many people disappearing on the road to the east, and here
was Mr Simsek with his open arms and enchanted village and
magic lorries, and that snug room upstairs. We looked suspiciously at our empty glasses of tea. All this from a little gleam in
the eye and an unexpected warmth in his greeting. We were
going to leave while we could.

Useless for Sayin to remonstrate that there would be no more cars that night; awkward for him to suggest that the village was safer than the countryside – since he had already scoffed at the suggestion of bandits with an impressive eloquence and energy; undignified for him to spread out his wares, tea, warmth, the bank, the beauty, tomorrow's traffic, before the accusing eyes of his colleagues, now sensing that their quicker-witted brother's plans were going wrong in uncomfortably public fashion, and half-jubilant at his downfall. Hopeless for us to comfort him and to explain that we were not 'toorestes' at all, that we were more like beggars, very far from the genuine, dollar-loaded article, that our whole journey was a hindrance to tourism, and not at all the sort of thing an up-and-coming tourist director wanted to be associated with.

Be calm Sayin, we told him as we left, be comforted. Only have patience and your empire is secure. Already the road behind us is groaning in anticipation of tens of years of travellers to Susehri; even now in the bedchambers of Europe and the Americas multitudes are labouring to conceive the unborn generations who will ensure Susehri a place in the suburbs of greater Istanbul. Only have patience. All this (or the approximate) we told him, but he was not comforted.

And despite his sad eyes and drooping shoulders, and general air of a man who has lost his way in life, he could not seduce us into Susehri for even a minute more. Not even for the jeering crowd surrounding him would we turn back. He profferred his friendship, and we dropped it without a thought. Our only concession was to correct the English of his 'Well Come' sign, and so speed him on his way. We did not owe him any more, we did not owe him that. But we placed him a little closer to the nightmare paradise he craved, we vandalised his notice board and so disposed of one aspect of his home's uniqueness. And if he ever managed to deal with the gang who surrounded him and to re-establish himself as the tourist-chief expectant, perhaps he would be grateful for that. We left as freely as we had come, and were well satisfied.

As we walked down the hill from Susehri there were bright red roller birds in the trees, and the little soldiers in the orchards carried only spades and whispered closely together and pinned roses in each other's smocks. They sported them like medals. The police house had a stork's nest in the roof, and a boy tending goats pissed triumphantly from a hillock above the road. The day's heat pressed the fragrance of the fruit trees and the wood smoke into the lanes we passed down, a dog barked idly in the distance. As dusk fell in the woods beneath the village we stumbled among a herd of cows and exchanged a greeting with their herdsman. Was there a small cry from the street above, as of a bank clerk being lynched? It was the quietest, softest evening of our trip.

Sitting in the dusk when it had grown too dark to throw a rock in the air and aim pebbles at it, waiting for the lift that we knew would save us from returning to the village, we were disposed to look on ourselves as though from England. Our friends, thinking of us in Anatolia, waiting beside the highway to India, hitching a ride on the trading traffic that for centuries had rolled ceaselessly to the east, and seeing us sitting at the side of this leafy unpaved lane, would say that we were lost. And the thought kept us happy for some time.

At last, an hour after sunset, when we could no longer see even each other, although huddled together for warmth, we got a lift. The driver of a Landrover, a farmer, who was going fifty miles down the road to Refayihe that night, came bumping out of the night and slowed down. There was room for everyone. We climbed gratefully into the back and sang to him. He gave every appearance of enjoying our performance and sang right back at us. His rather tuneless wail blended uneasily with our over-strident, many-noted howls. At one point we climbed out for a meal, and made our way through the bitter night into a log cabin with an earth floor, where an old man offered us bread and yogurt. The Rat did his swiftly improving impression of a chicken, and after a few minutes we were sitting by the hut's open fire, eating fried egg and unleaven bread sandwiches and swigging mugs of chay by the dim light of the oil lamp.

We had decided despite the cold to sleep by the roadside to make sure of getting one of the dawn lorries, but the farmer, when he realised this, was horrified, and insisted on taking us into the village of Refayihe and discovering, on our behalf, the time of the first bus to Erzincan, and a place to sleep. He explained that sleeping by the road was out of the question since there had been heavy rains and portions of the highway might be swept away overnight. The room he showed us was on the first floor of a cafe, and we had the choice of separate beds in the corridor or the privacy of three beds in a room off it. The corridor was dominated by a stench coming from the dark hole at the end, and in the light of one grimy electric bulb it had something of the air of a Crimean hospital. For a few pennies more we chose the room, and Barry produced a makeshift crystal set. Sleep came to the unmistakable accents of the B.B.C. overseas service. We thought of Sayin Seyfettin Simsek, and we hoped that his B.B.C. subscription had not been stopped.

Bound together like pilgrims, like spoilt priests in search of a church, we were not over troubled by that day's betrayals. We had relied on each other's capacity to be unreliable, it was part of our ability to keep travelling. Our freedom gave us privileges and we took them gracelessly. We moved among strangers without knowledge or money or friends. We came to this instability impulsively and with love. Like early naviga-tors we were still wondering that we could make a mark, that we could meet the essential demands of our passing surround-ings.

We were still accustoming ourselves to the unfamiliar idea that such places as Istanbul and Ankara and perhaps Katmandu, might be more than names on a map. Nothing was real in our minds until it had known us. Then it was real. When we followed a name on a signpost and found at the end of the road a place with that name, it still gave us pleasure. One never really believes that a place exists until one has been there. It was an unsuspected form of egoism, and one we looked forward to satisfying on each day of our journey.

It had been the softest day of the trip, and it would have to be paid for. If we ended the day elated we did not do so entirely easily; knowing, like good westerners, the retribution that would surely follow.

III Cauchemar

Eastern Turkey is noted for its water meadows and its fighting camels, but the valley we found ourselves in on the next chill morning seemed notable for nothing, not even the occasional lorry.

By oversleeping we had missed the day's only bus to Erzincan, so carefully disclosed to us on the previous night, and so we left the village on foot, escorted by some of that region's least welcoming schoolboys, stocky lads in Lenin caps who spoke good French and just enough English to say, 'You going now. Good.' There was a feeling of defeat about the day. The hobgoblin Simsek was active.

Out of the village the land changed colour. The sky and the stones and the streams grew grey, the weak sun showed high steep hills at either end of the bumpy meadows. One narrow road crawled across the valley, nervously clinging to the northern slopes. The great cleft was empty and silent. Nothing moved. At such a time, after such a night, one has the feeling that one is about to die. After all what else were we doing alone in this forgotten valley? It was too remote a place to figure in the reality of those who were going to leave it. The sense of desertion was too strong. We had obviously come here to die. The road ended among these grey rocks and sodden mounds, the pursuit was over, the journey complete. Somewhere in this dank concavity, a lost traveller's burial ground, we would find the Styx. Had the schoolboys been whelped by Cerberus? Apart from them nothing moved. Nothing moved because nothing lived. Did they, the Authorities, allow for mistakes? If we said we wanted to leave would they refund our lives? My water bottle began to leak.

It seemed hard not to leave Turkey when we were hoping to reach the Himalayas. We sat by the dead road for some minutes, the clouds chasing the sunshafts across the ground, and the only sound the steel trickling streams. It was intolerable to be forgotten into death, but that seemed to be what was happening. We were finding it harder to remember the world outside the valley, and clearly the world would be having the same trouble. Already we were losing a sense of our reality.

And then we realised that there was a noise, away to the left, a distant engine in the west. It echoed through the pass for minutes until at the far valley end, it became a little bright lorry. It became brighter and larger and buzzed louder. Its noise preceded it by nearly a mile and thundered around us like a promise. The pursuit was not over, here were the pursuers. They had found the trail, they were back. It would take longer to lose them, further, older, and we were rather glad. The world had not abandoned us to death. Simsek might prove impotent yet, and we existed after all. The mounds shrank, the grass turned green, somewhere beyond the village a cheated dog barked.

The lorry drowned everything as it approached, the last train out of Nagasaki, an individual sunray beamed on to its flaming reds and yellows. It was a Mercedes, a TIR truck, air-conditioned and customs-sealed, a non-stop express from

Munich to Teheran. Ann was placed at the apex of our party, her legs glinting like burnished spears. The driver responded in some style and did not steam-brake until he was almost upon us. He would travel a thousand miles in two days and he had room for three. Rat loaded up with Ann and Barry and we were alone again.

Travelling can become a drug. You begin to need more, and you need it again and again. You can see the end; it is the next town, or a break for lunch, or 'halfway'. But until that is reached you have to keep moving, and once you are there you soon find that resting is no help; you must be off again, and so you find a reason, you discover another place to reach, and the cycle restarts. Until the lorry disappeared among the low hills to the east, leaving us as we had been, but with the valley seeming to close in once more on our diminished party, we had accepted the incidents of the journey as they came. We had found a rhythm in the alternate waiting and moving; we were content to be carried east by those who chose to carry us, and to wait patiently until they presented themselves.

Now our journey had changed. The pursuit became warmer, we had to move faster. We were trapped in the first country we were to pass through, we had failed so far to cross a single border. It seemed as though the chase might end within days of beginning, as though we might never cross the first barricade. That would be a shameful failure. We were bound back through several centuries and across some thousands of miles, away from today and ourselves, a journey on a different plane of time. To be caught by those we were escaping within a week, without crossing a border, was not acceptable. In rage and panic we lost the rhythm which was supporting us, we accepted no delays and we would not rest. Somehow we had to rejoin the happy bands high up on the cushioned seats of TIR trucks. We had to keep moving. Later that day, out of the burial ground after riding in the back of a construction lorry down wide grit passes to Erzincan, we crossed a broad river and saw two overlanders walking together well away from the road beside the stream's flat banks. Had they shaken off the pursuit? Had they started earlier west? They were the last travellers we were to see until the Persian border. In our new haste to reach a place we could look back from, somewhere from which to count the miles, we withdrew from the surrounding country and those who lived in it. The only objects we noticed were metal ones, travelling east.

I cannot now remember how we explained to ourselves why we were undertaking this part of the journey at such breakneck speed. Teheran, where we eventually rested, was far less pleasant than many of the towns we passed through. But at this stage we were still behaving like commuters, with a subconscious timetable and a need to tick objectives off a mental list. Our preoccupation caused us to break a promise to visit the gaol in Erzincan and so we never met Robert Pontin who was in prison there and writing to the London magazine, *International Times*. Here is what he wrote.

'Dear Friends of IT,

Here I sit, surrounded by sunflowers, blue skies and hot sun in Erzincan, a Turkish prison in eastern Turkey. Apricots hang from the walls, dried by the sun.

In February, 1966 I was arrested in Kayseri, Southern Turkey, on charges of possessing 2½ kilos of hash. I was sentenced to nine years four months gaol. The judge said that I was going to sell "my own personal belongings", this was without evidence or proof that I was going to sell. That was 2½ years ago. With one-third taken off for good behaviour, I have three years nine months more to serve. Can anyone help?

Arsen Sinikcyan is an Armenian from Lebanon; in 1965 he was caught on the Turkish-Greek border at Ipsala customs with 13 kilos in the lining of his bag. The court took two months, he didn't have a lawyer, he was sentenced to thirty years. He appealed but the sentence was the same. With one third taken off he has 16 more years to serve. "Is there any hope?" "I wait for a pardon."

My Consul doesn't help me very much. I don't receive any books. I'm slowly deteriorating, rotting away, my mental image is gone.

Now remember, we don't receive an amnesty. What harm have we caused Turkey and its people? None whatsoever. We have not deprived anyone from life, from living. We have not thieved and killed. We have not raped and killed. These are considered serious crimes by humane minds. But not here, not in Turkey. These offenders receive amnesties, we don't. Why?

We are humans, isn't this insanity? Thirty years, twenty years in prison, an offence considered worse than murder. Can anyone help us?

Love to you all . . .

> Robert E. A. Pontin,
> Merkez Cezaevi,
> Erzincan,
> Turkey.

By the evening we had reached the last city before the border after a day of steady driving in a succession of lorries, sharing the truck space with families of peasants who used these vehicles as buses, for want of anything more reliable. They were habitually charged a small sum (whatever they could afford, for the drivers turned no one away), but we as foreigners were charged nothing. Rather were we helped as one would help a guest. The lorries had been hot and had taken great bounds across the eastern plains, lulling us in their steady motion from the panic that had seized us in the morning. Now in the evening in Erzerum, where we intended to pause for a

meal before travelling through the night on the last leg to the
border, we learnt that there was an obstacle ahead. We could
not enter Persia without a visa, and we could not get a visa at
the border. Instead we would have to turn towards the nearest
consulate, 250 miles away in Trabzon on the Black Sea, a
journey to the north when we were only interested in moving
ceaselessly east, an irrelevant pause in time while our companions continued unchecked in their flight, and our pursuers drew closer having trapped us once more, before the
first border, in the first week. We would get to Trabzon at
once, that night, in the first car that would take us. Travel
was our only relief from travelling; it was our entry into
Cauchemar, the country that had loomed ahead of us since
the grey hours in the valley that morning. The road there lay
over more mountains. Like Xenophon and the ten thousand,
we had been turned by hostile tribes and outlandish customs
towards the sea, and our salvation seemed to lie in ordered
flight. We unrolled our sleeping bags and somehow found
room on the floor of an American station waggon avoiding
the mud and the draughts, trying not to be sickened by the
vibrations and uncontrollable swaying. Perhaps nobody 2,400
years before had tempted Xenophon to delay his departure
with a suggested visit to the local brothel – 'the best in
Turkey, girls so fat you won't believe; and this is a good day,
the doctor examined last night' – but I am sure that if they
had done he would have been as regretfully resolute as we. Not
even fat Turkish girls could compete at that moment with
'the sea'.

The night bumped on, John as usual fast asleep; the car
climbing and turning interminably until, just past the highest
point in the road, on the edge of the treeline, it grew lighter
and we stumbled out to watch the dawn. We blundered
through the gloom, over sleeping dogs and through sweet thick
woodsmoke, to a delicate glass of clear golden tea, with bitter

dregs to cure the night's thirst, beside an early fire. Outside, in the cold air, raw, fatty meats hung on the wooden posts at the front of the hut, the coming day's flies frozen on to them. Already a few figures were stirring at the back of the room, looking around sleepily for the stoup of cold water and the tea. They were gangers and slept there every night in their working clothes, warm and odorous. As we turned to resume our journey the sun came up and we could see beyond the car, in the direction of the road's next twist, a hazy blue triangle between the steep, green-streamered hills. The sea.

A few hours later we descended into Trabzon, Xenophon's Trepisum, and repaired at once to the town *hamam*. It was a mouldy place, and we had to drive away a rat with our loofahs. The customer in front of us collected an automatic with his loose change, and when the Persian consulate at last opened the woman who dealt with the visas, pouring with sweat and half asleep, seemed to be an early case of plague.

'How are you travelling?' she asked. On foot. 'No one enters Persia on foot,' she replied, but stamped the passports anyway.

It was cool by the sea, sunny with no humidity. We almost regretted that we had not taken the coastal road from Ankara, although then we would not have met Sayin Seyfettin Simsek. On the other hand we would not have fallen into Yozgat either; next time we would keep to the coast. In any event there was no more rest by the coast than there had been on the plains. We burned for them, and for the border they were so determinedly withholding, and by ten o'clock that night we had recrossed the hills (something Xenophon never did : he, at least, had the sense to return to Sparta), and were sitting by the road in Erzerum, still without sleep and looking for a truck to the border, our obstinate determination to move eastward undiminished by the exhausting diversion.

In Erzerum we waited through the night, at first by the fire of an army picket on the outskirts of the town, where the im-

passive soldiers drinking their endless coffee regarded us in-
curiously and offered us none. We had been travellers long
enough to recognise this as a rebuff. We had come to expect
the gift of coffee as our right, and if it was withheld we were
offended. Later we moved to another pitch on waste ground
beside the town cemetery, a useful area since it was boycotted
even by the town dogs. John solemnly unrolled his sleeping
bag beneath the waste ground's only street lamp and went to
sleep. I kept awake by building a cairn (for sound tactical
reasons, we were still obsessed by the dogs). At about two a.m.
a van stopped and agreed to take us to a town nearly halfway
to the border. More asleep than awake we climbed in and
started to doze off and then noticed a strong stench from a
shape on the seat beside us. It was a bundle of blankets, soaked
in blood and vomit, and the dim light of the van showed that
the doors were also splashed with blood. The peasants explained that there had been an accident and the person who
had been bleeding was now dead. By way of illustration they
patted a shotgun. As an afterthought they added that they
would be stopping well short of their original destination, but
they would be most happy to accept payment for their kindness. Now. They stopped the van and we paid them promptly
enough, but reluctantly, hoping to avoid any impression of
unlimited wealth. As they looked at our rucksacks their eyes
glowed like 'Anticipation' in the old chocolate ads. The journey resumed. We decided, tired and fuddled as we were, that
they were quite likely to rob us and so determined to form
up in a defensive square, backs to the locked rear door, knives
inconspicuously to the front. A ludicrous staring match developed through the rear view mirror, our hosts whispered
incessantly; we agreed that if there were any false moves our
only hope was to lash out first. John then fell asleep.

I spent the rest of that journey in a state of outraged heroic
watchfulness. I was furious with John for sleeping and kicked

him surreptitiously into a few lucid intervals. The peasants started psychological warfare. They counted aloud in fluent home counties English, they summoned up a hunt which crossed the road ahead of us in vivid pink and white. Lights started to flash in the surrounding countryside and I had a clear impression of a group of renegade farmers, rustic wreckers trying to tempt our van into a large axle-breaking hole by the roadside. An attack was clearly imminent, John dozed contentedly on.

Finally the peasants stopped the van and motioned us to get out. They drove off with a civil wave and we were left in the pitch dark scarcely able to see each other. As we groped around for our bags, a light snapped on behind us, held by a man holding a revolver. He was the village watchman and he led us to a cup of tea.

It was the darkest hour, the whole village was asleep, but its night defence force was parading in the chay house, each in a crumpled homespun brown uniform with a little black revolver and three days growth of beard. Each seated behind a delicate glass of chay. Our watchman made his entrance with a flourish producing his two captives proudly and the room nodded at us gravely and offered us seats. Inside it was warm and dimly lit, two travellers were asleep in one corner; outside it grew no lighter, and we seemed to have stumbled at last off the modern map and on to another older atlas. Here were villages where people slept when it was dark and where the nights were like nights from childhood – long black intervals in the world's life, which one could avoid by going to sleep when one went to bed, but into which one could be terrifyingly thrust by an untimely awakening. One can become mesmerised by a map when one is travelling. No one takes the colours literally, and one should not take the lines literally either. Maps show only dots and lines and make no reference to the all-important dimension of time; so their lines are lies and should be ignored. Journeys through unfamiliar space are an everyday occurrence, conscious journeys through unfamiliar time are increasingly hard to come by. You have to abandon a time-table, for you must not try to regulate this dimension, and you must move at a pace set by events outside your control. You should be travelling slower than you normally do for in this way you become aware of the time and how it affects your movements and the existence of those you travel among. Perhaps most important of all you should be travelling in an area of the world where there is a different scale of time, where people are puzzled by the western attitude to time as something to be charted and rationed, or bought and sold; a place where not enough time has yet passed to smooth out the differences between one village and the next, between the villages and the towns, between the towns and the cities, and between the neighbouring countries and continents. For the first time our journey seemed to be through such an area. It had been plotted on a time map, not a space map, and the nameless villages in which we now came to several hours' rest occupied a prominent position.

Our companions having seated us and refreshed us began energetically, in friendly sign language, to misinform us of the various movements of trains and lorries on the next day – an event which they awaited with more confidence than we could summon. It seemed to me then that on a certain latitude east of Erzerum, the nights are eighteen hours long, and we had somehow to survive this painful interruption. The floor was very dirty but not too dirty. It was, however, too hard. Next door was the bakery, the baker was the only other man awake and at work, his furnace glowed, and, as the night-watchmen one by one slipped away into the freezing night and the temperature in the chay house dropped with each departure, we explored the possibility of sleeping in the bakery. There was no room. One could either lie in the freezing chay house or stand in the glowing bakery. Neither alternative was tolerable. John disappeared in the direction of the railway sidings and I spent the time walking from bakery to chay house and back again, the effort involved in this being an acceptable distraction from my weariness. Finally I can remember settling in a precarious balance on the edge of a tilted chair over the chay house's boiling samovar, this being the only part of the room which was tolerably warm, and thinking as I dozed off that if I lost my balance I was quite likely to fall forward on to the scalding metal. It was an interesting possibility but not one to keep me awake. I did not fall on to the samovar for, as the night dragged past and fatigue grew, my determination to keep travelling grew with it – the more tired, the more restless. The two conditions, fatigue and impatience, rushed towards each other like lines on a graph. When they met I hoped I would collapse.

At this point we had been two days and two nights without sleep, but although there had been other times when I had gone without sleep for longer periods, I had never experienced hallucinations. I did now. Why is not clear; John had slept almost as little as I had, and we were to pass another two days and a night before we did sleep, but he experienced nothing. He dozed slightly more than I did, but not enough to explain our differing holds on reality. From the middle of that night I had a continual series of illusions, and passed the hours in a state of half-consciousness. I could hold a conversation in Turkey with my eyes open, and in England with anyone I chose with my eyes closed. Both conversations were equally vivid; in London I conversed through a bright red haze, but my companions were no less real than the Turks. The people I spoke to were as close to me, their voices as clear. At the time I remember thinking that I must be dreaming both when I was awake and when I was asleep. It did not seem important which was illusion and which fantasy.

Just when I imagined myself to be on the point of collapsing into a happy state of unconsciousness, an interruption occurred. Another traveller, a van driver, had arrived and was demanding tea. Before he went to sleep he agreed to give us a lift to the border and signed to me to move our bags into his van. I walked out into the still freezing night, and threw the bags into the back of the van, disturbing slightly another man asleep on the front seat. Then I went in search of John. It was dawn and for the first time one could see how small was the village in which we had passed the night. As I returned alone to the chay house my new friend emerged, leapt into a different van, and drove off. He was possibly hopeful of having our bags and not us. In any event he was proceeding towards the Russian border and not the Persian one. Before my doubled mistake could become a trebled one, and so prove inconvenient, I retrieved our bags from the second van, again disturbing its increasingly irritable driver, and walked out of the village. On the way I had to cross a railway line and between the tracks I found John crouched over an oil drum and concentrating fiercely on the prospect of distant minarets.

Briskly we left that village, with its kind inhabitants and thieving visitors. It was another bleak morning, the dogs were too cold to move and the rocks with which we armed ourselves remained unused in our bags. About two miles outside the village we stopped. The mist was rising on the meadows, an orchard beside the road was still empty. Behind us the road wound towards the chimney smoke, ahead into some low hills – beyond which, God only knew how many days away, lay the Persian border. Hundreds of miles back in Susehri we had known precisely how distant the border was, twenty-four hours. Now, when it was perhaps only a hundred miles away, we knew no longer. Too many pessimistic estimates had proved optimistic. We had lost trust in our space maps; a time map could not be drawn before the journey was complete. To this ignorance we were now resigned, and in that sense our journey had still not begun. Away to the left a stork, or a crane or a heron, stood patiently by a pool waiting for a frog. The only noise was made by the frogs. They boomed from every puddle.

We stacked our bags in a neat pile beside the road and walked away in opposite directions. John to demolish, with a return of his fierce and irrational concentration, the wooden road bridge that was our only link with the border, myself on a frog hunt. Like the stork I stood over a pool and gazed at the tiny depression in the dark surface of the water that marked the frog's mouth. It saw me and it did not boom. Slowly the idea came that I might drop my knife into it. Maybe we could eat it. Were we hungry? I could not remember. I held the knife gently, delicately above the frog; would the blade slither off and be lost in the pool? Maybe I should leave the frog to the storks? I circled the pool thinking that the frog would take the opportunity to submerge. But when I returned it was still there. And it was gazing at me. Such perversity had to be punished; I aimed the blade. Beyond the orchard a child appeared over the hill, bound for the village. He saw the crouched figures by the road and made a great detour through the frog meadows to avoid them. The stork flew off. Shouting. It was John. My preoccupation had made me miss the only car of the day, a fast Mercedes. It stopped several hundred yards down the road beside his ravaged bridge. The frog had gone. Through the glazed air come John's fluent but idiosyncratic French. He seemed to think we were on a conversation course – no lift was worth all that energy. A light truck from the village drew up beside me and offered a fair lift. I toyed with the idea of proceeding independently, but no, I would play the gent. The truck driver became impatient while I shouted to John to hurry. Finally my Turks drove off. 'My God,' I thought, 'we've missed a lift halfway to the border and it's not yet six. He'll pay for this.' Jovelike I advanced down the road bearing John's bag for a thunderbolt.

'Do you realise,' I said. 'You've just made us lose a lift of fifty miles?'

'Shut up and get in the back,' he said. 'The Mercedes is going to Teheran.'

I instructed the driver to make it snappy and passed into a light sleep.

The last miles before the Persian border were passed in a half-wakeful and richly visionary torpor. Our driver was a Persian on holiday from the International School of Catering in Geneva. He had bought his Mercedes secondhand, and told us that it was a birthday present for his brother. There was scarcely room for me on the back seat among the pile of radios, record players, be-tissued silk shirts and suits, and similar indispensables. From within the soiled clothes in which I slumped over his cushions, it seemed to me that his life must be unbearably cluttered and accessoried. I pondered absently on how he might be helped to the desirable simplicity of one pair of jeans, a money belt and a rucksack.

It grew to be a blazing hot day and the road moved out from the chain of low hills on to a dusty plain inhabited only by goatherds and miserable looking detachments of Turkish soldiers. In the distance beyond the plains was the outline of Mount Ararat; beyond that was Russia. The plain must once have been the golden road to Samarkand. Good tank country. We drove on and on down the two track road, the main road, the only road, to India. Occasionally a vast off-white dog rushed, in absent-minded habit, at the speeding car. The pursuit had recommenced, it began to feel as though the border would no longer see us at rest. Teheran had been mentioned and was now the obvious, the inevitable, goal; the one we had *really* been thinking of. I began to wonder if we could ever pause in the journey and take stock. In one village NicB (that

was all we could make of his name) halted to take on water
and buy some plums. John consumed both enthusiastically and
I took keen pleasure in reminding him of the many consequences of eating fresh fruit and drinking unboiled water in
hot climates. He munched on contentedly. Nothing happened
to him at all. My own abstinence was as much due to inability
as caution. The machinery had ground to a halt. The mouth
would accept nothing, it was indeed almost too dry to open.
The eyes on the other hand were too hot to close. I was floating
inside an outer layer of skin which was firmly attached, inch
by inch, to my shirt and trousers. Within this double cover-
ing I could move freely into a more comfortable position, but
the movement was invisible. The skin remained attached to
the clothes, the clothes to the seat. Neither moved as I did.
The head, with sanded-open eyes, continued to gaze fixedly at
John's neck. After some hours NicB, whose one task on these
long empty roads was to keep awake, went to sleep. He did
this at sixty m.p.h. just before the only bend for miles. The
incident occurred during one of my more alert spells, and as
we approached the apex of the curve it became clear that he
was making no attempt to turn the wheel. At this point the
road was bordered by a high bank separated from the tarmac
by a broad shallow ditch. The car went straight down into the
ditch and up on to the bank. It banged from left to right, the
wheels on both sides alternately leaving the ground; finally it
steered itself off the bank, across the ditch and back on to the
road. All this while NicB had sat sleepily gazing over the
wheel, too startled to operate any of the controls. Now he
shook himself awake and proceeded down the road at a slower
pace, muttering inaudibly. Behind us a group of nomads who
had been crouched by the bend gazed after us, apparently
appreciative of our driver's skill. They were in exactly the
same composed attitudes they had assumed during our
approach, save that they were now standing rather than

crouching, presumably to get a better view of the smash. One could sense some disappointment in their passivity.

The road continued narrow and straight across the dusty plain. We passed a broken lorry, its driver crouched beneath it, a few children by his side. The children had a capacity to appear, like the flies, in the most deserted spots as soon as one stopped moving. At one moment NicB halted to sleep and I left the car. Away from the road the land reimposed its remoteness. It was not hard to imagine oneself lost where one stood; the heat haze magnified its distances and obscured its foregrounds. I hurried back to the road and dozed off in some shade. One of the children began to fan me and I woke as the car moved off. Somehow I scrambled in.

'Oh,' said NicB, 'you were out there.'

We never really took to each other.

Towards midday we reached the border and made our separate ways through the customs.

The Turkish-Persian border, on the road which runs between Mount Ararat and Lake Van, is a dusty collection of huts on a rise in the desert. The buildings are enclosed in a compound and to reach them the road passes beneath a high wooden arch into a stockade down the middle of which runs a chain. It is a satisfyingly visible border. The stockade was empty save for a few cannibalised lorries, and although this seemed to be the only customs post that there was between the two countries business was not brisk. On the wall inside the building there were pinned some rather tattered messages.

'To all fellow Gulhanes, don't stay at the Baghdad Hotel in Teheran, it is a hustle. Stay at the Amir Kabir.'

'Stay at the Baghdad Hotel.'

'Teheran is a drag. Kabul and Herat are just right.'

'Pete – this is the sixth of yours I have read.'

There was nothing from Rat; we imagined him, cocooned in

his TIR truck, no doubt at that moment drawing into the outskirts of Teheran the *urbs mirabilis*.

At first there was no sign of the ghost army of travellers who had left these messages. Where were they, our 'fellow Gulhanes', whom we had imagined festooning the route from Istanbul to Delhi, swarming on and off bullock carts, meditating beside mud huts, the halt refugees from the 'Smart lad wanted' ads? Slowly during the early afternoon they began to assemble, limping in mainly from the east, usually alone as lifts are easier that way. They were tanned and sick and content, and they settled around the stockade as though they had been there before, and began to exchange 'the news'. An exhausted German tottered in and collapsed beside us; he enquired anxiously about the Turks. Were they still the same?

'The same?'

He patted his bottom.

'Oh. Yes.'

'Ach.'

On his last journey through Turkey he had spent a night on the floor of a public lavatory and had woken to find a crowd of Turks gathered round his huddled, well-haired form trying to puzzle out his sex. 'I don't know why they bothered. For them it was an academic point.' He moved off, bitter and apprehensive, towards the welcoming Turkish officials.

A little green car bumbled into the compound bearing Selwyn and Nora. Their clear English voices tinkled up and down, apparently bartering with the natives. Money, as Selwyn later explained, was no problem. Nora was a highly merchandisable commodity, and he sold her two or three times a week. Nora, who looked a healthy, country girl, beamed enthusiastically and confided that it was probably because she didn't wear a bra. Selwyn, jovial, told us that the whole business 'creased him up'. He offered us a tin opener. 'Nora only goes for wogs,' he said apologetically. Beyond him the Persians were opening negotiations with Nora. She had put a rather literal interpretation on the principle of 'divide and rule'. On the other side of the compound we could see NicB grappling with his native customs officers. One of them, a gentle ancient with a habit of removing a full set of false teeth in mid-argument, had wheeled out an electronic device and was examining the Mercedes with its aid. His main concern seemed to be over the size of the tip.

For a short time it was almost as though we were once again below the Blue Mosque, on the roof of the Gulhane. We read the notice board and exchanged information about rest-houses and routes and where in Greece or the Gulf we might get a good price for blood. Somehow our companions had lost the rather theatrical air that had accompanied their beads and far-away look in Istanbul. They were purged of pretensions by the achievement of their survival out here on the road. Tattered modern descendants of Richard Hannay, they were beggar forerunners of a pacifist empire-building race, preaching the gospel of Kim; people who had decided that the only way of escape was down; a band who had failed to 'fix-it', in their terms a uniquely honourable failure.

Somewhere near Erzerum, where the pace of our descent had quickened, the fleas had left us. Now for an hour or so we sat in the shade in unirritated repose and talked of the road. The western attitude to travellers as people 'up to no good' was gradually disappearing. We found ourselves among a more recently nomadic people and hospitality was here endemic. This was not because of a greater generosity. It was a relic, like most human characteristics, of necessity. If you refuse hospitality to a desert nomad he dies.

An immigration officer, with a rifle on his shoulder approached, carrying a tattered blue book. 'William Cowper wrote: "Knowledge is proud that he has learned so much,

Wisdom is humble he knows no more," did he not? What did
Cowper mean?' This took some time to explain.

Eventually NicB disentangled himself from the customs man
with the false teeth and we set out for Teheran. He was looking thoughtful. He said that the car, consumer goods and tip
had added up to nearly £300. As we left, the customs officer
was shuffling back into his shed stuffing a large wad into his
pocket and the German was playing with a Persian soldier
by pretending to jump over the chain. It seemed to be some
form of virility contest; the soldier who wore no socks and
had holes in his boots was disinclined to handle the German
but looked as though he might shoot him. The rest of the
travellers were waiting for a lift and munching 'hamburgers',
wads of flat bread filled with uncooked meat balls. Selwyn
and Nora seemed to have opened an appointments book.

It became hotter as we descended on to another camel plain
and John and I relapsed into an uncomfortable stupor. The
only clear memory I have of that afternoon is of passing one
of the many army posts and seeing an officer wave languidly
at the speeding car. Long after we had forgotten about this
NicB decided that it might be more circumspect to return to
the post. As it turned out the officer had only been waving,
but he was charmed by our driver's eagerness to oblige. No
there was nothing he wanted, none of his detachment needed
a lift, he would be delighted for us to continue our journey.
One of his soldiers produced a snake in a bottle. We admired
it and drove off. Somehow one would never have thought it
necessary to turn back for a stray Turkish army officer; one
would have expected him to have shown surprise if we had
done so. It was an unreassuring change.

Towards the end of the afternoon we reached the city of
Tabriz, about a quarter of the way to Teheran, and the largest
town in north-west Persia. Here NicB announced that he had
friends and would probably stay the night, an entirely unsatis-

factory decision evincing, as it seemed to us, monumental selfishness when Teheran was scarcely a night's drive away. The fellow clearly had no persistence thus to break off when his task was so nearly complete. We arranged to have a meal and meet him again when he had made his decision. Tabriz was not a very attractive town; it had a shabby modernity, with new office buildings and great holes in the pavements. While in search of food I remember that we were approached by a self-confident man who spoke incorrect English loud and fast in a German accent.

'Who were we? Where were we going? Why? Were we students? Why not? Why did we not wash and shave more often? Tonight we would stay in such a hotel, isn't it? Oh yes we would? What you mean "get stuffed"?' We became abusive and he had to leave.

Looking back on the incident, it seems likely that the man was one of Persia's thousands of police spies, his air of seedy authority did not suit a curious passer-by. At the time John thought that he might have been attracted by the sergeant's stripes which he still carried on the arm of his jacket, and so, while we chewed rather miserably through a kebab, he removed the stripes with a razor – an operation that attracted an enormous crowd to the window of the kebab house. After the kebab we both wanted a baclava or its Persian equivalent, and in pursuit of this I went into the kitchen, there to tread on the cook who was prostrate on the floor at his prayers. He was very nice about it. Back at the square another crowd was gathered and at its centre I imagined I should find two such freaks as ourselves. Sure enough there were Sam from Islington and his mate, Pete, last remarked separated and distraught by the roadside somewhere between Istanbul and Ankara. Sam seemed by this time thoroughly tired of the crowds which he everywhere attracted, and became so aggressive that it seemed quite possible that the people's curiosity would turn to something more threatening. In an attempt to embarrass them away he broke into a capering dance, flapping his arms and chanting. Surprisingly this worked and we were left to drink chay on the pavement and read the *Kayhan International*. NicB was so late that we had almost given him up when he arrived just before midnight to show his friends what he had brought back with him from Europe. He was perfumed and freshly hosed and it became clear that he would be staying in Tabriz. One of his friends said that there were some army furlough buses leaving overnight for the capital, and we were grateful for the offer of a lift to their departure point. The buses were crowded and the seats small. Clearly we would get no sleep on them. After some bargaining with the proprietor it was agreed that we should travel the five hundred miles to Teheran for five shillings each, less than the cost of staying in the town. The soldiers were clearly not overjoyed by our presence but they eventually made room for us. During the night I can remember belabouring John, who was as usual in a light doze, with a cigarette packet which I had torn from his shirt pocket. One of the soldiers having watched this performance with mild surprise returned it to him. At intervals the soldiers would join in a shouted prayer. Once I looked from the bus and saw parading by the side of the road massed ranks of Wrens, stiff and neat and rather disapproving. Nora had apparently made more impression than I had realised. Towards dawn, the third to be thrust at us without the decent preliminary of sleep, John muttered, 'Am I home yet?' This struck me as conventionally funny and I bared my teeth in an attempt to make haha. But my lips cracked with the effort and no sound could mount the chipped throat. I merely succeeded in making my mouth bleed.

Morning showed a changed countryside. We were on the busiest road since Ankara and it was lined every 200 yards or so with armed troops, as though for a state visit. But there was no state visit in Teheran that day. Just routine precautions for restraining the subjects of the King of Kings from greeting him too passionately. Towards midday our bus drove into the city centre, a place we had been straining for since the moment in Erzerum when the way had suddenly grown longer. As we drove slowly towards the bus station through crowded streets we passed Pingo on foot, well on his way to Bombay, a western female bearer carrying an enormous rucksack trudging a few paces behind him. His shades were firmly in place, his fuzzy black hair was as carefully dishevelled as ever. One knew without approaching him that he bore the fruity smell of a man who has been hitching for a week or so, and that he was playing complaisant host to all varieties of friendly Asian creatures. One knew this without approaching him because of the lovely used look of the man, and because they parted from him on that crowded footway with remarkable eagerness.

'Pingo. Pingo,' we shouted and waved to him. And he after his initial surprise at meeting other than abuse from a military vehicle, waved back. The soldiers looked pleased. Their two freaks knew the freak on the pavement. The creatures could evidently communicate. 'Pingo,' they murmured to each other. They had discovered the English word of greeting.

That was the last time we saw Pingo. Teheran proved too crowded to reveal his hole in the few days we were there. The city was, as Wontan said, 'a wretched scene'. Wontan was Australian and now spoke little English, and that in a curious, muttered form. He had left Melbourne four years ago and was trying to make his way back. He had no money and begged for his food. His tangled hair hung down below his shoulders, he wore what had once been khaki trousers torn above his twisted knees. Above the rope holding them he had a black leather waistcoat. That was all. No beads, no staff, no trim shoulder bag. To beg he cupped his hands, he was without need of a bowl. He had been staying free at the Sikh Temple,

which traditionally offered free hospitality, but in Teheran
the temple had decided to withdraw this privilege from those
who were not Sikhs, and since then Wentan had been sleeping
in a field on the edge of the city. He walked in every day to
beg and to observe his fellow overlanders from a distance. He
seldom spoke to them, he seemed to have as little in common
with them as they had with tourists. He told an improbable
story of losing forty kilos of hash to a thief, and pursuing the
man all the way from Brussels to Greenwich Village where he
was arrested on suspicion of being connected with the murder
of President Kennedy. We left him limping down the street
to pass some brooding hours in the Hotel Amir Kebir. It
seemed quite likely that he would never make Melbourne. He
was not strong and he had lost his European appearance. He
would have no edge over the professional beggars of India and
the south-east.

Outside Teheran there was a notice which said, 'Welcome to
the Iranian capital. We hope you have a good trip.'

'At least,' said Rat who we found in the Amir Kebir, 'somebody is trying to make us feel welcome.' There was little other
sign of it. The grubby *bouquinistes* displayed copies of *Smith's
Urology*. The streets were full of old Hillman taxis whose
drivers harboured overtly murderous intentions towards unkempt westerners. On the walls of the British Embassy's reception room there was pinned a photograph of 'Raymond Pattison, missing.' Whether Raymond Pattison was missing or
found, whether he was alive or dead, he has evidently so far
shaken off his pursuers as to persuade them to advertise for him.
To that extent his journey had been a success; he had escaped.

That is the other reason why I remember Teheran. For all
its supercilious hostility it was the place where we regained
the rhythm of our travels; in reaching it we were at last able
to accept the possibility of staying awhile at more attractive
places. Somewhere on the way to Teheran we had lost track

c*

of the days, and no matter how we tried to remember there was one which we could never trace. And looking back down the road to Tabriz there was no sign of pursuit. We had left the west and our lives there. We had earned a place by the road, we were tempered to withstand the uncertainty of our days. Our first slight hardships were a badge of honour in our band. We had reached the far border of Cauchemar, a sleep would carry us across, and wash away the time we had passed there as though it had occurred in another man's life. Tomorrow we faced a new road, where Simsek's writ no longer ran.

IV The Citadel

The Hotel Amir Kebir, which we had been recommended as far back as Istanbul, was in the street of the tyre sellers; in that part of Teheran consecrated to the motor, and more especially to the greater motor or lorry, and most particularly to the tyres thereof. The inhabitants dozed in the tractor tyres, and washed in the saloon tyres and walked around upon shoes fashioned from motor cycle tyres. If, when you left the hotel, you wanted to avoid the reception desk, you just leaped into a heap of tyres piled up outside the first floor balcony, and the proprietor never saw you again.

The week before we arrived the Amir Kebir's only rival, the Place Across the Road, had suffered from one of the sporadic police raids and been temporarily closed. So most of the capital's overlanders were now staying in this hotel which resembled nothing so much as a delapidated YMCA, and the glass-topped tables and tiled floors contrasted strongly with bare feet and mantras. The proprietor, despite the periodic exits over the balcony, maintained his belief in the old-fashioned courtesies, and every half-hour the guests were served with free cups of tea. Despite this generosity it was generally agreed that Teheran was a very great waste of time. An international police conference on drug smuggling was about to open, and it loomed over that little hotel in the tyre market like an execution.

An international police conference was bad news at the best of times but one called to discuss drug smuggling merited a specially warm degree of apprehension, and one called in Persia doubly so. Only one British citizen (in contrast to Turkey) was at that time serving a jail sentence in Persia – five-and-a-half years in the southern jail of Zahedan; and he, being a Khan born in Malaysia, was not an effective symbol of the prosperous northern races' over-enthusiastic response to the delights of indigenous eastern vices. It was however pretty clear that this international police conference might inspire the national police of the Peacock Throne to extra zeal in their daily investigations. Clearly it would be in their interests that something should be seen to be done immediately. For a week at least cannabis must not pass between Baluchistan and Azerbaijan. They were policemen of their word, and they made many suggestions as to what they should do with such American and French and German and British and Japanese visitors as ventured beneath the Peacock Throne with so much as a curl of a substance. Just after the conference ended they made it a capital offence to be caught smuggling drugs into Persia. (Later, we were to read in *The Times* of 15 December, 1968, that 'Ten people, including three army officers, were executed today at Jamshideyeh army garrison, Teheran, on charges of smuggling heroin and opium. Their bodies were handed over to relatives for burial.')

The only man in Teheran who really seemed to be enjoying the place was Sam, who was about to make his right turn to Kuwait and Arabia. Since he was leaving the sheepskin trail it behoved him at this furthest point east to purchase one, and the last we saw of him he had been bargaining for three days for a really choice brown lambskin which had been dyed and embroidered and was on offer for a mere one thousand six hundred rials. Sam had got the merchant down to eight hundred rials and was still going hard. He only had two hundred rials to spend, but the coat seller did not know that, and Sam was looking disgusted enough to offer only fifty. The coat seller thought the offer of eight hundred was something remarkable, indeed that Sam was something remarkable.

I next saw Sam two years later at an English pop festival. It was a warm day, but he was wearing his coat. . . .

As we prepared to leave Teheran there was news that the roads ahead were closed by floods. Nobody could move out, and rumours had also begun to spread of an outbreak of cholera on the eastern border which would close it for six weeks. Six weeks in Teheran was out of the question, there was only one thing to do; consult Her Britannic Majesty's Consul. And we joined the queue.

Along the road we had heard of some hair-raising interpretations which the various consuls placed on their duty to help travelling nationals when those nationals turned out to be hippies. British consuls were apparently no better disposed than the rest, but in Teheran the officials, though bored and condescending in the way of all consuls when asked for help, were at least conscientious. They were chiefly contemptuous of their charges' blatant ignorance of the lands which they had come to admire, and perturbed by their blithe acceptance of the risks which came from travelling dumb and unaccompanied among the primitive tribes in the north and east. Persia was in any case an increasingly hostile country to overlanders. The traditions of its hospitality had been severely strained. Many Persians now asked 'why do these strong, rich people come here to live off us? Why does the West despatch these infidel beggars with their blue eyes and the habit of talking to our children?'

In the view of the Teheran consul the best course for the hippies was west. The year before he had repatriated seventeen citizens, only one of whom had been sick. He could buy us an air ticket home, and then the government would dun us for repayment. He was not allowed to lend people money for journeys to the east.

All this the consul explained patiently, even a little wearily to the queue which sought his advice, and which was marshalled outside his office by a khaki-uniformed Persian, who maintained a most remarkable climax of astonishment at the turn taken by the appearance of his master's visitors.

The consul dispensed his advice like an astringent ointment. There was something disturbing about the ambience of his office, with its neat leather furniture and paper knives and blotters and files and desk. It was an unsettling vision of order in the chaos of our days. But when we stepped out into the street again, the vision faded. The blotters had changed nothing; our departure, though based on better information, seemed as difficult as ever.

Beyond this tedious city were the mythical lands with enticing names. Wiser heads, like Ulysses, would bind themselves to the embassy railings or stuff their boots with wax, and proceed no further. They would not brave the tigers of the Caspian rain forests or the wolves of Parapamissu. They would never meet the Pathans who brandished the captured Lee Enfields of 1880, and perhaps still treasured the shrivelled remains of some more personal accoutrements of those members of the Suffolk Regiment who were killed in the passes to the south of Kabul and whose names are cut into the walls of St Edmund's Abbey in Bury. But our restlessness was renewed by the sight of the wild men on their way back, and by a reminder of the uncertainty of the road. 'Teheran is a drag. Kabul and Herat are just right.' The man who had written that in the Turkish customs shed had been right about Teheran. It seemed the moment to verify his estimate of the Afghani towns.

The wild men said that the cheapest way to get to the border was to take a pilgrim bus to Meshed and then look around. One of the big coaches would get there in twenty-four hours, non-stop, just an occasional halt to water the driver. At this time of the year there was a fair amount of traffic from there to the border, and they thought that it might well be possible to get a free ride for the remaining two hundred and fifty miles to Herat. The wild men said nothing about cholera or floods and so we accepted their advice.

The next day we loaded up optimistically enough and went down to the bus station to buy some tickets. The next bus to Meshed was scheduled to leave in a few minutes. Would it leave on time? Oh no, it would not leave on time, it would probably not leave for several days. There were terrible floods, Meshed was cut off from the west, departure might be delayed, who knew how long? No, it would not be possible to refund our tickets. Why should they be refunded? The buses would certainly leave just as soon as the road was open. That was to say when God had decided it. And the only thing for even an infidel to do was to possess himself in patience and wait for the Lord. That was clear. That was also intolerable. We wanted to go now, and we wanted our money back before making a further attempt. We could not afford the luxury of a long-term future investment in a seat on the company's Teheran-Meshed run.

Psst, said the bus clerk's assistant who had had a thought. There *was* just one driver in the depot mad enough to ignore the will of Allah and risk his conveyance over the flooded roads. This man knew of a hazardous mountain route which might or might not be flooded. Would we like to go with him?

You betchar, lead us to him.

Apparently men were even now leaving their normal tasks and forming great queues all over town although they had no business in Meshed at all, and would certainly return the moment they arrived ... or so said our guide.

Our bus, which was painted bright yellow and orange and was of a hybrid Germano-Persian strain, pulled out of the compound in some style to the accompaniment of shouting from the dutiful queues, and the curses of the tout. Nothing for him even though he got us on the last bus to paradise. There was a feeling that Allah, having approved the rest of the assembly's decision not to square up to his floods, was brooding over what to do about the one man who was defying him.

And there was one detail which gave us reason to believe that fortune's next retribution might come at any time: we were seated on the cross-benches at the back of the bus in those places exclusively reserved for the Persian women and children. There was nowhere to which we could tactfully retreat. We remembered the consul's warnings about the religious fanatics who still believed in the evil eye and nursed a strong distrust of foreigners and an inhospitable tendency to treat them as scapegoats for any misfortunes that happened along. If they were strangers that was bad enough, if they had blue eyes that was considerably worse. Blue eyes were evil; if a cow sickened or a child was burned after a pair had passed by, their owner might be pursued to render account.

For some minutes we conducted a vigorous disagreement about how we had got into this situation, where we were likely to end up that night, whose fault it was (quite forgetting, for the time, that we were at the mercy of events and just following history along the road). The dispute continued well beyond the point of reason or experience and was followed by an hour of determined silence broken only by a youth immediately in front of us. Now and again he popped up over the back of his bench and beamed the beginning of an announcement. 'Bobby Kennedy kaput.' He ran his finger across his throat and disappeared still beaming. Apparently the ex-President's brother was not popular in Persia.

Silence was broken when the Iran-Peyme's orange monster, now well off the main road to Meshed pulled up for lunch. We were in a mountainous area between the capital and the Caspian, just ahead of us was the peak of Damavand rising out of a plateau that lay around it, the highest mountain in Persia. Most of our fellow passengers started to pray. The women sat beside a shaded pool, whose green water cooled them. Lunch was not good. Having established that we were English, those in the cafe studiously ignored us. We were reduced to dry biscuits, which in the heat that was building up were not sustaining. We remounted and prepared ourselves once again for the suspicious scrutiny of the men up front. We were behaving ourselves.

Outside, the scenery grew craggier as we climbed. The road kept pretty level, but the country around it climbed and dropped in the most abrupt way, forcing our path to loop and wriggle around its outcrops and gulfs. While we remained on a level course the peaks would soar almost directly above us on one side, and then plunged into the dusty abyss below us on the other. At the foot of one such plunge we could make out a white Mercedes which had evidently rolled straight down, right way up, before splitting itself on a boulder. There were no indications as to who had been driving but it did not look to have been there very long.

Later in the afternoon we were forced to halt, for the floods had burst across the road. The surface had been torn away and a channel, thirty yards wide and several feet deep, had been formed; it was filled with rubble. Soldiers were there, and a great number of lorries, the whole of that day's traffic, was waiting on either side of the torrent. The soldiers said that it might take several days to repair the track and that the best course was to return to Teheran.

Fortunately it was not only in us that the thought of half a day's steady travelling west induced a deep despair. The brotherhood of drivers waiting by that high rift for the army to do its work were well aware of the distinction between them and the millions of their fellow countrymen who could not drive. They were Drivers and they were not to be turned back by a small matter of a river thirty yards wide. The fact that they were up in that primitive pass at all meant that they were determined; there were bonus payments, and family reunions and, above all, reputations at stake on this pass. The army could say what it wanted. This road had to be opened before dusk or they would be a discontented body of men.

And so, gradually, it became apparent that there were two task forces at work on this matter of a bridge. An official one in grey uniforms who moved in columns and by numbers and extremely slowly, with much countermanding and consulting – and even some slight attempt at overall direction. And another, much less numerous and without apparent organisation, composed of men in white shirts who toiled like mad beside the foaming water in the dry heat of the pass, raising a choking cloud of dust, for the ground was already, pending the next cloudburst, as dry as bone.

Fortunately, to prevent any technical or social disputes, the anarchic drivers and the plodding soldiery worked a few yards apart; the drivers, as befitted their non-official status, were a few yards upstream where the current was stronger and the abyss deeper and the stones larger. But none the less they worked to more effect, and this was possible quite apart from their professional and individual pride, for a very good reason.

Above them, and on the far side of the torrent, there was a slight rise in the ground, a gentle hummock, and its summit was crowned with a few stunted trees. These trees provided the only shade on the far side of the workings, and so the women stranded on that side had climbed the hillock, and were grouped closely in the shade. At that distance their veils were lowered and, in their fine robes, they formed a silent host, a shimmering crowd of watchers to inspire the workers below. And since it was clear that if there was to be a bridge that day it would be because the drivers had spurred on the army; and since it was easy to take the view that the ladies were watching your efforts in particular if you were out of uniform and therefore more capable of making an individual contribution, it seemed likely that those ladies proved decisive in deciding the race. In any event it was not long before the anarchists in white shirts had established a distinct advantage. And as soon as this happened it behoved the rival officers to change their role, to become obstructors rather than bridge builders, to impede and delay, and so retain their primary position in the course of events and, hopefully, in the attention of the ladies.

But it was too late. Few powers on earth can delay a motionless Persian lorry driver two weeks out of Hamburg with the smell of the home kebab in his nose and only thirty yards of raging torrent between him and sleep. The anarchists' bridge was completed, declared to be complete, and officially condemned within a few seconds. The drivers announced their intention of taking their vehicles across it at once and the officers announced their immediate intention of arresting anyone who dared jeopardise the future of the road, the pass, even the Peacock Throne itself by doing any such rash thing. Were there those present who would defy the Imperial army and its long-term plans for rejoining this temporarily truncated Imperial highway? Who would be so rash as to take an articulated twelve-wheeler across those few flimsy stones and risk having all swept down on to the assembled company?

There was a great clamour among the anarchist engineers, and from both sides of the flimsy causeway pantechnicons rushed forward for the honour of being the first to defy the Imperial order.

The passengers gathered on the banks, the two engines roared, the giants advanced for combat. Even the soldiers dropped their shovels and gathered to look. At the last minute sense prevailed. One of the monsters gave way, though without prejudicing his right to go next by god, and the other advanced on to the misshapen and disjointed platform. All those downstream rushed upstream to avoid the impending smash, and then the driver, sensing that the bridge was truly, anarchically, sound, accelerated – and was safe. The divide was crossed. There was a roar of applause. Our driver, our Hector was summoning us and we had to leave the curious crowd that had gathered around. Perkins signed a few last autographs, au revoir, auf wiedersehen, salaam: Our bus was the next across. As we passed over and round the steep curve in the road we saw the ladies fluttering from their knoll and remounting the west-bound buses. The soldiers laboured on.

(In January 1970 avalanches again closed the road. On this occasion one hundred and fifty people died, including thirty-six who were found frozen to death in their seats in an Iran-Peyme coach. One eyewitness said: 'The entire mountain on the opposite curve collapsed with a noise like that of an earthquake ... sweeping with it one bus, two lorries and a car. They rolled down into the ravine like matchboxes, and within minutes the ravine was filled with snow....')

After crossing the stream the atmosphere in the bus underwent a marked change. Confidence was renewed in our driver, and he appreciated this. He was a small man, 'snowy-banded, delicate-handed', whose scent reached from one end of the

coach to the other, who fenced daintily with his great wheel
and blew passionate kisses at anyone who looked in his direction. As our mood changed so, abruptly, did the country we
passed through. One moment we were ascending another
dusty incline with nothing to be seen except empty hillsides
and deep ravines, the next we had turned a shallower bend
and found ourselves in thick mist. We drove through this for
a few minutes and then it cleared to reveal dripping green
trees and flat fields. Everywhere the rain poured on to the
lush ripeness of the good earth. Where before one had not
been able to see for the dust and the haze, the view was now
obscured by the low clouds and the sodden vegetation of the
Caspian littoral. We were among the northern rice paddies,
the richest agricultural land in Persia. Nowhere had been quite
so wet in the fifteen hundred miles since Istanbul. We cheered
up at once.

This was our Hector's secret. The sea route to the north
where they knew about floods and relief rain. Where the
earth was like treacle and the men and women who worked
on it were amphibious creatures who spent much of their
lives up to their chests in mud and emerged like so many
decorated nuts in a chocolate factory, until the rain washed
them clean from their breasts to their waists and from their
skirts to their knees. Beneath the mud they wore brightly
printed linens and headcloths, wet weather coolies without
the straw hats.

Until early evening our route ran by the grey waters of
the Gorgan estuary, by the caviar fisheries of the Caspian,
which produced the finest caviar in the world. 'Caviar comes
from the virgin sturgeon,' sang Perkins as we left the second
sea which we had glimpsed on this officially sealess journey
from the Sea of Marmaras to the Indian Ocean.

Tea was produced here, and cotton and coal and wheat, and
possibly cane sugar, but all we could see were the rice paddies.

As we climbed again towards rising ground to the south, night fell and we caught the last distant view of the inland sea. We turned back to our companions.

For pilgrims, they were a light-hearted crew. Apart from the comedians in front, with their endless 'Bobby Kennedy ... urrgh', there was a chubby beauty of sixteen who had dropped her veil at an early stage and spent much of the time mournfully ogling the evil ones in the back. The evil ones could only regard her as some sort of religious *agent provocateur*, bound as she was on this journey to the holiest city in Persia, and violating so shamelessly the essential modesty of her religion. In front of her there was a carefully-tended priest, in one of the seats of honour. He sat there, a vigorous man looked after constantly by two women; cushions were brought to him, he was plied with raisins and sherbet; his admirers, evidently set on getting the full blessing of their pilgrimage, treated him like the prophet. The other passengers seemed to find this sycophancy contemptible and made up for it by pointedly ignoring him. The priest noticed this and responded to it by extending his cordiality to them all the more warmly, forgiving them for the homage they failed to pay, and noting it for some auspicious moment within the mosque when his position would allow him to obtain satisfaction.

Beside us there was a handsome woman who spent much of the trip being inconspicuously sick into a bucket. Her veil was lowered perforce, but by this time all the women had lowered their veils and revealed their beauty. Many were of the traditional Persian type, fine light features, clear brown skins, dark eyes. None wore the supercilious expression which, on the unveiled streets of the degenerate capital, so often spoilt their appeal.

Towards nightfall the outrageous chubbiness in front redoubled her eyes and her efforts. And she was no longer pressed by the two ancient female relatives beside her to comport herself decently, nor did her father, sandwiched as he was between wives at the front, turn and glare at us with quite his former ferocity. Worse, one of the ancient females was also allowing her veil to droop a little, and was that a welcoming gleam in her rheumy eye, was she wiggling a cracked index finger in our direction?

The coach thundered through the night, and this journey, begun in doubt and recrimination, took on an epic stature. The bus was our citadel against the cold we drove through, its passengers our countrymen, its provisions at our disposal, its driver our city king. We were sheltered from the heat of the day and the cool of the night, the children could sit on the knees of the evil ones. Chubby-chops changed places with her gran and leant towards us, her plump ripeness within grabbing distance, her stare ever more hypnotic. If this were the west ... but it was not. She must be a *pro-vocateur*. Hastily we pretended sleep.

Towards midnight, having passed by Alexander's wall and reached the feet of the remaining hills between us and Meshed, we stopped for a meal. Outside the bus it was bitter and we were grateful for the warmth of a big room with a fire, and meat and bread enough for all. As we settled to eat, another bus drew up outside. It was heading west and it disgorged a most curious body of people. They were led by an old man in short trousers and a khaki shirt bearing a large jar of instant coffee. He was followed by two ladies in flowered dresses, woollies and floppy hats and then by a number of young girls. The party proceeded to order boiling water and to prepare their coffee and tinned milk before scouring a saucepan and cooking a meal of baked beans and sausages from a tin. One of them produced a medical box and handed round supplies of enterovioform; presumably because she thought the air was polluted. The girls ate all that the old man put before them but could on no account be pressed to accept even a crumb of our bread. We had crossed the path of the Australians abroad.

The driver, an Englishman, was outside wrestling with his engine. He was the only person in the party who reassured us that the rest were real. Further back in the mountains around Meshed he had collided with some animals and he was naturally anxious to reach Teheran before the question of blood money could catch up with him. He had twelve hours to go before he could consider himself safe, but his main problem lay in persuading the colonel, who was the group's self-appointed leader, that there was any risk of delay at all. The colonel knew better.

The driver knew better too. It was after all his job to take coach loads of westerners (at £150 a head) from Calcutta to London, and this trip was proving to be among the more in-teresting. They had been delayed for two weeks in Pakistan because of the cholera outbreak and had finally doubled back to Quetta, and thence by way of Kandahar and Herat, had crossed into Persia from Afghanistan instead. In Meshed several of the Australian girls had been stoned because they had gone too close to the mosque, and this had provided heavy ammunition for the colonel about the lack of recon-naissance and proper escorts. Then there had come the colli-sion. The driver knew that if the owner of the dead beasts ever caught up with him he would have a family feud on his hands. Failing a generous financial settlement, or an attempt to exact an adequate repayment at once, it was the usual practice to imprison the driver. Settlement could sometimes take several months.

Convincing the colonel of this likely chain of events had proved impossible. Regular stops for nescafé and baked beans were to continue, and as he waited for those inside, the driver sweated with his engine and cast nervous glances back for pursuing herdsmen from the east. None appeared, and eventually the colonel emerged and ordered a general embarkation. His lady companions followed him aboard and with a great crunching of gears the coach drew hurriedly away. We were alone once again in Asia.

Of the rest of that night I have little recollection. Sometimes we were woken by the cold and knew that our commander was dozing – for no other was authorised to fence with his great wheel. On the whole he was tireless and we kept moving, all of us warm, unveiled women and snoring priest and evil ones in a jumble of canteens and bowls and children sprawled around the citadel. Perkins was carried off to a place of honour beside the driver and was only able to regain the comparative roominess of the back bench by threatening to play his mouth harp. At some time in the night the chubby lady passed us a rose. Resolute cowards to the last, we passed it right back.

The morning broke sharp and jagged and found us making our way across another flat, dry plain. But it was an inhabited plain, with turtle doves hurrying towards its horizons, and foxes, buzzards and waxwings crowding by its trafficless roads. Once we saw a wolf, but never the tigers which Thesiger had assured us dwelt in the forests by the shores of the Caspian Thesiger, with his succinct views on motors, would have explained why we saw none. We were now beyond the Kuhe Shah Jehan and Kuhe Binalud. We had left behind the floods and the earth tremors which had threatened in Teheran, and there was nothing between us and Meshed except the time remaining to be spent in this desert. After twenty-four hours, towards mid-morning, we drew into the holy city, our own citadel still celebrating its accomplished journey as though in carnival. Our Hector had kept his word, he had defied Allah and proved his eagerness to enter God's gates. We were almost across Persia.

That thought proved the destruction of any slight chance

we might have had of staying in Meshed. After the days of enforced idleness in Teheran we could not bear to stop travelling. How could we when we still did not know whether this journey would ever be completed? Perhaps Wontan had once had such definite plans as ours, and where was he now? It was essential to cross now and reach our next destination. Once we had bidden farewell to our fellow citizens of the Iran-Peyme Meshed took an unwelcoming aspect. The Persian ladies pulled up their veils and hurried away for all the world as though they had never seen us before. The driver joined the raucous groups at the bus station. We were freaks again. We remembered the girls who had been stoned – infidels after all were put to death if they went to Mecca : what might the proud Persian get up to, to rival that barbarity here in the last resting place of Ali, the prophet's friend? Besides, if we moved now before the sun got too hot we might even reach Herat, the first town over the Afghani border, by night. The country between us was flat, the distance was little over 200 miles and it was desert all the way. Nobody stopped in a desert, one ride would take us there. It seemed a foregone conclusion.

With these plans already forming, as prematurely as ever, we climbed into a cart whose driver, we were assured, would put us on our way. Somebody wrote out the directions for the cart driver, and then had to read them aloud to him. We set off across the town pulled by a scraggy horse with an open weal down one flank which the carter kept moist for the flies by the continual and precise use of his whip.

He left us beside the road on the far outskirts and passed on, waving in the general direction of a street to the right. Sure enough between two crumbling mud walls there was a building with buses outside it. Not a grand Iran-Peyme sort of bus station, but a humble place whose buses had started life as lorries. It was now the heat of the day and nothing was due to leave for an hour at least, so we joined the dozy group sitting in the dust beneath the shade of one of the lorries and prepared to defeat our hunger with sleep.

As we dozed we dreamt that a voice from above addressed us. 'Would you like some scrambled eggs while you wait?' This coming from our collective subconscious seemed both tactless and unnecessary. We knew exactly how much we would like some scrambled eggs while we waited, so we muttered and twitched and settled ourselves once more in the dust and found the question repeated, this time in more forceful tones.

His name was Hussein and had we not been so tired we might have noticed the sign outside his cafe – 'Breakfast and Teas'. He sped away on his mobillette and soon we were installed inside eating great numbers of eggs and bread and drinking mugs of chay. After a while his friend, waiter and assistant cook turned up, a boy of seventeen called Reza who was also a reporter on the local paper and a student.

'What do you study?'

'Mathematics.'

'Where, at school?'

'No. At Cambridge.' He was going there next year with the only scholarship in Persia. Hussein also wanted to leave the country and find work in Europe and be near his friend. Could we help him in this? Did we know of the best place to earn money in Europe? There was also the question of his visa. Without a scholarship to Cambridge he needed an authority to leave the country, and this would cost him 2,000 rials – more money than he was likely to save in ten years. Already Reza looked bored with the subject of Hussein's visa. He had decided that it would never materialise.

They put us on the first bus, which went only as far as the border and we said goodbye to them regretfully. Reza accepted a copy of *Kim* as part of his essential preparations. Hussein waved a despondent farewell. Like the Turkish conscripts he found the contrast between our travels and his immobility frightening. He was clamped to this town and this age for as long as he could see. He was thirty years old and had no prospects. He had just begun to appreciate this.

The bus which went all the way to Herat had left the day before, and this one, by comparison, was in the second class. We crammed in beside a dozen goats and waved good-bye to the city of Ali and our only two Persian friends in an odour of dung and good wishes. The area we now passed into seemed to be one of the forgotten corners of the world, and in no danger of suffering from a tourist boom, but it was to be one from which we were to have considerable difficulty in escaping.

If we ever destroy the ozone belt with an accumulation of burnt-out waste gases and the water evaporates with the heat of the sun, the world for a few years may resemble the semi-inhabited dust bowl which lies between Meshed and Herat. To a westerner the area seems incapable of supporting any life and is one which would never be inhabited by any sensible man with the strength to drag himself out of it. But, as the earthquake which struck just after we had passed through showed, many people live and die in this wilderness; they mostly inhabit widely scattered and miserably poor hamlets which in the heat of June are barely distinguishable from the surrounding emptiness, and they support life by selling each other fruit and vegetables and by bartering for necessities in a primitive economy which allows no more than a tolerable number of them – mainly children – to starve to death each year.

The towns and villages were lifeless, exhausted places in that choking brown heat. Each seemed built on a similar pattern, perhaps two squares connected by a long shanty road, each square constructed round a centrepiece on some Imperial theme – a stone statue of the Shah gazing impenetrably into a glorious martial future, or a grotesquely large wrought-iron crown, usually dominated the stunted trees and the stagnant pool. Again and again the people's devotion to their ruler was recorded, but his reciprocal interest in them was less evident.

(It became more evident after the earthquake of 1968 which destroyed whole villages in this part of Persia. 'At least 10,000' people were said to be killed and many thousands more made homeless. On this occasion the Shah visited the area in a helicopter.)

The towns had little water apart from that supplied in the central pools. There was almost no shade. There was quite clearly no medical treatment. We saw one child who had a sore on his lip which had spread across most of one side of his face and turned septic. A squirt of antiseptic cream in the first week of infection might have cured it at once. Another was blind because his eyelids were swollen and bleeding and covered in flies. Eye ointment is very likely available in the palace. There is a hint in Persia today of that appalling contrast between the lives of the rich and the poor which led so few Russian workers to regret the news of the brutal murder of the Imperial family after the Revolution.

Everywhere we drove there was *one* example of Imperial interest: the army. This border was clearly not one of the crack postings in the empire, and judging by the competence of some of the officers, this was just as well. We passed one captain whose car had broken down in the desert and, an echo of that first day in Persia, our bus driver stopped although he was not requested to and although there were already two lorries helping the officer who owned it. It seemed that the officer had had a puncture and was unable to change his own wheel. There was a certain aggressive satisfaction in the manner in which the two drivers took him through the intricacies of changing the wheel on a modern Rootes saloon. Few words passed between the men; inside the car the officer's haughty wife sat bad temperedly waiting; we thought that she was beautiful, and she made her opinion of us equally clear.

A scorpion scuttled across the road under the bus. Nothing else disturbed the baked silence. Later we stopped in one of the dust towns for a meal. The driver and passengers disappeared into the back streets. We sat beside the pool which had some shade and consumed yogurts and bread. It was not a pleasant place but it was a better one. The town's lovers came and met here in the heat of the day lying side by side, dabbling in the pool, murmuring to each other. They were all male, the boys quite young. One ten-year-old was not provided with a partner. He came upon us suddenly. What was left of his nose had half rotted away, one side of his face had been burnt and there was only one wild eye. Seeing our startled expressions he hid this face in his hands.

The bus reached the last town before the border and turned around. We climbed on to the roof to retrieve our bags, and were put on our way by a cosmopolitan hunter who had joined us with his wife and family and deer rifle somewhere along the route. The cosmopolitan pointed up the dusty street to a police post and said 'Afghanistan'. We could hardly believe it. Even if this did not seem the ideal way, the Khyber Pass way, to approach the country, there it was at the end of the street, a name that was as appealing as Nepal.

We left the passengers getting together their sticks and carpets and the old woman who had smelt so foul, still with the veil over her face, still suckling her grandchild; and we set off up the road and found that it was not Afghanistan at all. It was Karir, just the first of the many police and army posts dividing the two countries. The heat had by now become stifling and everywhere we moved we raised a blanket of dust. Nothing else, not even a dog, was in sight. It was 12.30, there was only the line of wooden houses and the heat and the silence. When we raised a sleeping policeman in the visa office

and said 'Afghanistan' all he could say was that the last bus
left yesterday. Would there be lorries? Oh yes, perhaps, in a
few days. Sometimes there were two or three. Sometimes none
for several days. Was there anywhere to stay? Here in Karir?
A good joke that. No, he did not think there was anywhere
to stay.

A noise suddenly exploded down the street. It was a motor
cyclist. A German lad. And then another one. Empty pillions.
Yes, they had come from Turkey. They were going to spend
the summer in Kashmir and the winter in Goa. They had
stayed in the Amir Kebir and they too had read the notices.
True their pillions were empty, and were they sorry they could
not take us. A question of springs and petrol. Sorry man, and
they passed up the street into the dust haze guarding Afghanistan, leaving behind them the appalling silence and a renewed
impatience with the heat. There might not be any more like
them for a week or two.

The only good thing about the town was that nobody at
that time seemed to be worrying about the cholera quarantine.
Possibly news of the outbreak further south along the Persian
border had not yet reached Karir's sleep-drugged policeman;
it seemed more than ever imperative to break into Afghanistan
as soon as possible. How would our predecessors, the political
agents and military attachés, have managed it? Those playing
the great game. A reconnaissance seemed in order.

Further down the Persian side of the street, since the policemen would not let us move in a due easterly direction, we
found an empty compound. It had an arched wooden entrance
and a courtyard beyond. There was a great green pool in the
centre filled with carp and goldfish, and it was not quite empty
after all. Someone seemed to be throwing stones into the pool.
Further peering revealed a boy in a shady corner throwing the
stones. Behind him was an ancient and gaily-painted lorry.
The only vehicle at that moment in the town. It had a wheel

off, but it was loaded with boxes and crates and rugs, and it was very evidently an Afghani lorry. Nothing like it had been built in even the remotest parts of Persia. Underneath it was an Afghani mending the axle. An enormous man in a nightgown whose face still haunts me. We called him Jake.

Neither Jake nor the boy (who said that he was from Pakistan) would understand our suggestions, so we returned to the police post and demonstrated with the officer there.

Why had he not told us about Jake's lorry, clearly bound for the border and Herat?

Oh they had known about Jake, every policeman in the area knew about him, but there was no question of suggesting that we ride to Herat in his lorry. Jake could not be recommended: 'He crazy Afghani.'

For a start had we examined the vehicle? True it had once been a Bedford but there was an enormous and quite unsafe teak superstructure added to it which was likely to tip the whole vehicle over. Then there was its mechanical state. Apparently there was no one alive who could remember big Jake completing the journey between Karir and Herat in less than two days and one night. A breakdown always struck, and the inhabitants of both towns confidently looked forward to the occasion of big Jake's death out in the wilderness when a breakdown coincided with a sandstorm or an unusually cold night. Big Jake had no family and bets were being placed on which town would have to pay for this vast man's funeral. And then there was the question of customs delays. If we had passed this way before we would know that the most usual place to discover big Jake's lorry was not, despite his grotesque indolence in Herat or Karir, or despite its grotesque mechanical state on the road between the two, but, owing to his grotesque dishonesty and lust for rials, parked outside one of the customs posts between. Had we considered this? The baggage of anyone accompanying him would be as thoroughly searched.

And if it was at a Persian post and we were carrying cannabis ... The officer smiled.

And then, as a final deterrent, there was always the question of price. The policeman did not suppose that we had actually got as far as discussing that with big Jake yet. The driver was a competent bargainer. The question of price was never raised until he had made it clear that he was quite unable to carry passengers anyway. Did we still want to go with the night-gowned Afghani?

No, we most certainly did not. But, there was the question of our feverish impatience to move on; and the question of the impending cholera quarantine; not to mention my impending stomach cramp, brought on by an urgent need to use the police facilities swiftly followed by a sight of them; the two combining to induce a violent and piercing sphincteral pain. The officer seeing our hesitation said that he thought he could persuade us against travelling with the big Jake. If we cared to accompany him back to the compound he could with advantage point out certain aspects of the windscreen. ...

It was no use. Within half-an-hour we were sitting up beside Jake in his cab, lurching at about ten miles an hour over the desert pot-holes, jammed in with the Pakistani, the three of us on one seat while the big man spread himself over the other half of his cab, occasionally leaning down to take a long happy suck from his massy hubble-bubble.

'Certain aspects of the windscreen' had indeed been interesting. None of the original glass was left, and in its place Jake had installed a thick yellow slab of cracked house glass that rattled hideously in its sellotaped mount at each lurch of the lorry. We had been taken over the nicer points of this death trap by a friend of the policeman in Karir, a man who sat by himself outside the compound and whistled cheerfully. He was introduced as the latest of Jake's ex-mates, and he had the air of one who has just discovered that life has redisclosed its promise. Over one thumb he wore a grubby bandage which concealed a cut that had nearly severed it, and, as he was happy to emphasise, this had been caused by the windscreen behind which we now crouched, shades nervously in place, waiting for the inevitable stone to chip off some long yellow splinters.

The bidding with Jake had been complicated but brisk. He held all the cards anyway, and the severe contractions which forced one of his opponents to negotiate from a curled-up position in the dust at his feet gave him a clear advantage. The policeman was an indifferent translator, the Pakistani seemed chiefly concerned to ensure that we did not replace him or encourage Jake to increase his fare. Jake had refused to take us, thrown our bags heavily on top of his preposterous load, told us to be off and demanded a price of 200 rials for the 100 miles to Herat, all in the space of five minutes. Utterly defeated we had clambered in gratefully, and were soon shuddering down main street with a resigned police officer waving goodbye and assuring us that we would undoubtedly be back sooner than we thought.

That border was a prolonged business. We left Karir at about four o'clock in the afternoon and at eight that evening we had still not crossed it, but were only at the first of the Afghani police posts. On the way we had passed a succession of Persian forts, constructed alternately of mud and iron. Some had thin tin battlements with men crouched behind them. Sometimes a flag drooped in the airless light. At the last of these we had been approached by a customs officer who had confiscated the Pakistani's transistor, and had become so infuriated with the man's protests that he had nearly detained the Pakistani as well. Jake just beamed. It was a matter of indifference to him whether this passenger was detained or not. He had already paid his fare. We were in a different case. He shepherded us through the checks and restored us firmly to the bench beside him. We had not yet paid. Not yet. Jake fixed on us a threatening insincere smile, and once again held out his great fist and rubbed his fingers together.

'Later, Jake, later. At journey's end you'll get 200 afghanis.'

'Rials.'

'All right, rials.'

Our last contact with Persia was suitably authoritarian. In the middle of the desert, with nothing before or behind except the dust road there was a camouflaged tent. A grubby red and white flag was stitched on its sides and there was a bus heading for England parked outside it. The tent was the first sign of the northern cholera control. So far the soldiers were only stopping westbound travellers. The people in the bus had just been told that they would have to wait for three weeks. There was no arguing with the soldier from the Persian Red Crescent. As far as he knew there was no cholera in Afghanistan, but he had had his orders, and the bus stopped here.

We were waved through and just hoped that Jake's lorry did not break down before it reached the first Afghani post. It seemed unlikely that we would ever be allowed to return to the police compound at Karir. The passengers in the bus sat up as we passed and looked at us hopelessly. For all they knew they were in for three weeks right here, alternatively freezing and stifling, with nothing to see except the occasional gazelle. But we were still moving, even if only at a bumpy ten miles an hour, and their predicament left us untouched.

The first of the Afghani police posts was a welcome relief. We reached it in the evening, Jake's lorry having managed to put up a record time without breaking down. On one side of the road there was the customs control where the lorry was to be unloaded and thoroughly searched. On the other was the police post and health office. It was a water hole and we decided at this point to part company with our driver. He would certainly demand the full exorbitant fee and so we would have to be tactful. Our bags were still perched on the top of his

load.... The first thing to do, by a display of eagerness to help
the customs, was to separate the luggage from the area of
Jake's physical control. Next we would have to throw ourselves on the mercy of whichever official looked most likely to
stand up to Jake. Fortunately the business of examining his
load was likely to take some time, and we recovered our bags
while the big man was offering round his hubble-bubble. On
the far side of the compound there was a rest-house, and for
some hours we managed to keep out of Jake's way, but well
after dusk, his examination complete, he decided to continue
his journey and, in his big-hearted way, he came to tell us so.
At that time we were both asleep on the rest-house dining
table on which we had been served a meal and had then passed
out. Had it not been for the exhaustion we would undoubtedly
have got into an argument with two beefy short-trousered
travellers coming from Hong Kong, one a South African, one
from Belfast, who were holding forth with some vigour on
the subject of filthy woggy countries. For the moment they
were very useful. When big Jake loomed up in the twilight
and started to hector the two sleeping forms beside them
(which they had at least been able to establish as originally
white) the Ulsterman and the South African had taken it very
badly, and we woke to find that Jake's demands for our immediate return or prompt payment were being resisted by two
muscled strangers.

The line of their objections to Big Jake seemed to be very
much a development of their earlier reflections, but this was
clearly not a moment to compromise our unity with semantics.
Big Jake's great hands were working with alarming energy;
once he realised that there was a possibility that we would not
be paying him it was extraordinary how fast the insincerity
of his earlier smile was replaced by an honester expression –
simple hatred.

He shuffled round the table towards us in the gloom. His

flowing nightgown did not seem to obstruct him one bit. The
South African and the Ulsterman looked as though they
might delay him for a little, but they were not moderate men,
and an international incident was sure to be provoked, and
we would have to pay in the end. With barely a shout about
the need to fetch reinforcements we were out of the hut and
across the compound with all the speed our heavy legs could
get together. Big Jake was right behind us moving swiftly and
with commendable fluency for a man of his bulk. There were
barely two hundred yards to run but it was time enough for
the chase to revive all the childhood nightmares of pursuit and
the inability to run away. The uneven unfamiliar ground, the
pitch darkness broken only by the tiny distant lamps of the
customs officers' quarters, the unwilling clumsy response of
our legs, the grunts and thudding from behind us as the massive lorry driver, doubtless more familiar with the course, began to gain.

So much for the chase fantasies of the journey, here was the
reality of pursuit. We were fleeing for our very rials and we
could scarcely run.

It seemed that we burst into the customs officers' dining
room with Jake's horny paws at our necks. Exhausted we collapsed on to the official carpet. Playing the game strictly by
the rules (as well he might considering that he was completely
within his rights), Jake thumped to a halt by the door.

The lieutenant was seated on the floor dipping into a bowl
of food and surrounded by the more personable of his servants. 'Good-evening gentlemen,' he said, 'may I be of any
assistance?'

For the time being Jake was effectively thwarted. The customs officer would hear nothing of such a preposterous fare,
and with a token payment of twenty rials he was dismissed.
The lieutenant then devoted himself to our comfort. Had we
inspected the hotel? Yes. Unfortunately it could not be re-

commended very highly. Right. Where were we planning to sleep? Dunno. Could he suggest his own quarters? With certain provisos – he could. Splendid. He would supervise the erection of two beds at once. Clap clap and enter two more servants. After a certain amount of bustle and ordering about it became apparent that one bed was to be placed in the spare room across the corridor, one in the customs officer's room. Rearrangements; thoughts of bribing the servants; offers to sleep on the floor, which the lieutenant was able to advise against owing to the scorpion problem. Evidence of squashed scorpion on the wall produced with a flourish. Outside there came the only reassuring noise of the evening. The mighty grinding of big Jake moving from first to second gear and setting off into the night, in the company of a lone Pakistani who seemed to be in some danger of suffering from 180 rials worth of temper.

Perkins installed himself with graceless haste in the one bed in the spare room. The customs officer called again, and again, to see who had lost this desperate game of musical beds. Could he persuade us with a little Mosarr? Mossar? Sure enough the strains of the 'Jupiter' Symphony were drifting across the corridor. No. Well then perhaps some coffee? No. We secured the door and I rigged up some uncomfortable arrangement with bags and chairs.

Sleep came accompanied by the mournful tones of the lieutenant who had by now made his way round to the window. Hashish? Would we like some hasheesh?

The next morning we were out of the customs house and back across the compound into the police post at a smart pace. The lieutenant did not compromise the dignity of his office by pursuing us in broad daylight, but judging by the muffled noises coming from behind his door he was in no shape to contemplate anything so violent as climbing out of bed. Mosarr had given way to the near tuneless wailing of his private band.

Like Richard the Lionheart, who travelled nowhere without a troop of choirboys, he was cultivating his reputation as a music-lover.

Without Jake's lorry the compound seemed to have shrunk in the early morning light. The burning heat of the previous day, and the stifling heat of the night, had both gone. Instead there was a light cool sky and a warm breeze, too weak to raise the dust, strong enough to be refreshing. All we needed was water sufficiently warm to wash off yesterday's clogged filth and life, even in this barren border post, would for half-an-hour or so, until the sun regained its strength, become quite supportable. In the middle of the compound beside the stones which distinguished the edge of the dust road from the edge of the dust desert, under a solitary tree, there was a water tap. There was no hot water anywhere, so cold would have to do. But the tap ran from a tank on the roof, and it ran warm. We splashed about under it with happy cries for some time while the servants of minor officials patiently formed a queue.

Sitting in the shade of the stunted trees, getting dusty again, while we waited for the health officer to arrive. Sitting there from long after dawn and wondering what to do if the health officer treated us as generations of British immigration officials had treated eastern arrivals, clamouring to climb on to our fresh green lap. When he finally appeared, he dallied, he took our time and toyed with it. He wandered out to the tap and splashed himself a little. He transferred sheaves of crumbling paper from one chipped office to the next, he examined our appearance from a distance, he summoned a runner, he drank some water and he examined us from a lesser distance. It was *our* time that he was consuming, slowly and luxuriously and blatantly so that we could see him at it. We did not have his time to consume in return. He had months to deal with us. He lived here. We too were made to have nothing to do and nowhere to go. We too had to spend the day sitting in the com-

pound trying to keep cool and we were still sufficiently agi-
tated by the sense of time passing to resent the health officer's
indifference to it.

A dormobile appeared on the shimmering western horizon,
and swayed through the heat towards the compound and towards the trees which provided the only shade and under
which we sat. The first eastbound travellers, apart from ourselves, for twenty-four hours. We greeted them like brothers
and explained our need for a lift to Herat. They pointed to the
back of the van already crammed with a similar crew. They
could take no more. Considering our plight mere overcrowd-
ing seemed an inadequate excuse. We considered lying down
in front of the dormobile to delay their departure but remembering the customs pasha this might be a risky move. Just
then our luck changed. Rat climbed out of the van, and the
immigration officer sprang to life. He would see us at last.

Inside the cool walls of the health office there was an im-
mense gloom. The officer sat cross-legged on the room's only
carpet, waiting and relaxed and quizzical; prepared to read
our papers. Nobody was going to bother him in this room; he
had it organised. By his side on the carpet was a little pad of
blue ink and a rubber stamp. If he applied the stamp to the
ink and then to our health papers the man at the barricade at
the eastern end of the compound would allow us to pass.
Otherwise not. He was working this week, and that was why
there had to be all these rules. The room was thick with flies.
They crawled all over us and all over him, but he never once
brushed them away or gave any sign of noticing them. They
had been crawling over him for some years. Slowly he stamped
our papers, and we were free to go.

Outside again, the compound was empty once more. Nothing moved on either horizon. There was nothing to do but sit
on the steps of the rest-house with Rat, doze in the heat, and
wait. Once I woke to see a great red petrol tanker drawing

away towards Persia. High above us towered its barrel sides, and sitting on the top, roasting in the sun, frying on the steel, were the Ulsterman and the Afrikaaner. Blistering away without complaint. Still showing the wogs.

We dozed most of the morning, and woke feeling hungry, and glanced over to the water tap and saw our next ride.

V A leech beneath the bandage

The trip from the border to Herat was made in the back of an unsprung German newspaper van. It took us across the remaining miles of desert. Somewhere out on the road we passed big Jake, who had managed his usual breakdown and had had to spend the night there. We waved to him and he bared his teeth at us. His Pakistani passenger did not look too happy either. Eventually we drove straight past the town and had to retrace our steps. It seemed a good omen. Herat was the biggest community for thousands of square miles, and yet it was so inconspicuous that we could drive straight past it.

At one moment, back on the steps of the rest-house, we had been dozing away the day, with every prospect of another twenty-four hours fighting off the customs officer and not so much as a hint that there was a bus due for a week at least. At the next we were blinking at the vision of a sharp little van with a tall man in jeans and leather cowboy boots fussing round it, adjusting its engine and reloading its supplies, talking with a second man who had tied a bandana round his head. Two men in a big van and going our way. It restored one's belief in the gods.

Their van was an Aladdin's cave of water jars and tape recorders and tins and sacks. We caught a glimpse of blankets and a clothes line. It looked cool, and was there just a hint of something in the air, something fresh splashing out into the heat, something that smelled interesting.

A twitching of the nose, a new alertness about our inspection. There was some sound or some smell inside that van, something that stirred distant memories, there was an air of expectancy around it as though the curtain was about to go up. And then there came a noise, drifting across the compound to the rest-house steps, like a temple bell through the midday heat, distant and soft through the stifling silence. Two people inside the van were talking quietly, and laughing. Two girls...

The pack was over there immediately, Rat out in front. Excuse ME mister, just one moment GUV. Going to Herat sir? Got any room for two or three more? Just for the hour or two to Herat. Sure you can manage it? Grovel grovel grovel.

Tremendous, a million thanks, here's some money for the petrol, and, by the way, what's that you got inside there? Wait and see.

And we did. For half-an-hour or more, while the two tall Americans soaped and polished and cherished the outside of the van so that it twinkled and beamed, and the two bodies inside splashed around in their private tub and sprayed a little eau de cologne and put out more flypaper, and generally made their house fit for our arrival, we waited to meet Rose and June.

Rose and june rose and june, blonde and scrubbed – and just the thing for travellers' despair. We dusted down our dirty hands on our dirty trousers, and hopped from foot to foot, and said howdy ma'am and tried a callow smile. Little poems about rose and june all the way to Herat, quietly of course in case any one heard.

They had bought the van in Marrakesh, and shared the

driving all the way. Most of their supplies came from an American NATO base in Turkey where they had gorged themselves on beans and clams and sausage and stocked up well before leaving. Normally such bases are not a haven for travel-stained buccaneers living off cannabis and brown rice and in irregular domestic circumstances. But in this case the issue was confused because Rose's father was a retired army colonel in Wyoming, surviving there, although he did not know it, without his army pass. His army pass was in the shoulder bag of his lovely daughter, and thus the multi-coloured paper van was able to spend a week parked behind the PX, trading cannabis for coke and steaks. When they had crammed to bursting they bade farewell to the sorrowful soldiers and slipped out just before the military police could satisfy a paternal interest in this festive truck, its all-American crew and the colonel's pass.

We climbed up in front, and Rat slipped in behind where the girls were, and where travelling was a matter of stretching out on the bed planks and trying not to squash anyone too hard. Just as we set out it occurred to the buccaneer in the bandana that although they had come all the way from Marrakesh and crossed countless borders, they had never yet jumped one. The Afghani border seemed like a nice friendly one to jump. The barrier was up, the guard was asleep and instead of waking him we accelerated right past. And then the buccaneer had jumped a border and we could drive out into a dust storm thick enough to discourage pursuit and conceal what Rat was up to in the back, and make our way to Herat.

Somewhere on the road the van hit a sand bank at fifty miles an hour in nil visibility. Somehow our driver kept his foot on the brake, but the three in the back were bounced from floor to roof and back again like peas in a steel whistle, and they spent the rest of the journey trying to reconstruct the sleeping quarters and to separate the molasses from the flypaper, and we all felt that that had served Rat very well indeed.

Herat is a small town with three or four avenues of stunted dusty trees and one close-shaded street. Its grander houses stand around watered court-yards, it has an ancient and sacred mosque with minarets of mud, and a less sacred new mosque with towers of porcelain and gold. There are horse carriages with brass mudguards and velvet canopies and there are water-boys with big wooden scoops who damp down the powdered streets from the gutters they drink and wash in. At first sight Herat is a poor place, but for refugees from the wilderness it very quickly becomes a paradise, a paradise of fruit trees and corn gardens and spice shops, of water and shade.

Meshed had been a holy city and a place of pilgrimage for Moslems from all over the world; Herat is not a holy city, but it has become a place of pilgrimage for the scattered parties of overlanders exhausted by the road which leads to it and the spasmodic efficiency of the Persian and Turkish cannabis squads. It was the first country on the long road west where nobody bothered to enforce the drug laws.

When animals are forced to trespass on each other's territory and crowd too close, they sicken and grow perverted and eventually they may die. They are within the critical distance, and like dogs which have come too close they must fight or run. It is a concept which any inhabitant of a developed western city finds easy to understand, but it has a corollary in the solitude of the road. People, even townspeople with their neurotic need of each other, their thirst for approval and their fear of silence, can grow quickly perverted if they are too much alone. There had been little enough contact on the road, and we had begun to turn morose and eccentric and unpredictable in temper. The society of the paper van was a first hint of the returning warmth of companionship. Herat was a confirmation of this comfort, it was a destination, a place to stay and talk. At the least it would give us a chance to catch breath and listen for the footsteps behind; at most it might prove the place where we could break into the prison of obsession for the east.

There were only two hotels in town. The Behzad was in the middle of the broadest street, with shops clustered round it like parasites and rooms costing three-and-six a night. As he showed us to our room the proprietor begged us to lock the door carefully whenever we went out as the room next door was occupied by an Afghani; we thanked him and later discovered that 'the Afghani' was the hotel receptionist.

The hotel was full of those who, like us, had struggled along a solitary path from Istanbul and were anxious for the news. There were also small parties going the other way, usually suffering from dysentery and sometimes recovering from hepatitis. In India the heat was now reported to be building up to its annual peak, and those returning were questioned anxiously.

How did one travel from here? Did it take long? What did it cost? Was that good or bad? What were Indian immigration officers like? And the food? And so on and so on. The main subject was the heat. Even here apparently in the middle of the Afghanistan desert it was cool after the Indian plains just before the monsoon. For the first time it seemed possible that the heat stories might not have been exaggerated after all. The other topic was disease. The dining room came to resemble a hospital ward with its continual talk of bowels. Dysentery was apparently unconnected with chance encounters or careless hygiene. It was everywhere. As an example of this we were told of the procedure in a western embassy at Kabul. Here the staff did not have to worry about a contaminated water supply, they had their private deep well. The water was pumped from this and stored in a sealed tank where it was chlorinated. Before it was used it was carefully filtered and most people then took the additional precaution of boiling it as well. Finally it was seldom served until it had been adulterated with tinned fruit juice. The staff of the embassy still succumbed to dysentery regularly. The story was related with some satisfaction by one of those who had recently dealt with the embassy. Among the overlanders the disease was endemic. Few people bothered to dose their water, arguing that it was better to resign oneself to an immunising attack of the germ and so ensure a more normal life. The flaw in this argument was that as one travelled one came across an apparently endless variety of strains of infection, and so natural immunity was evasive. Instead one developed a stoic outlook, and eventually even a moderately severe attack might not interfere with one's travelling plans.

Later, after supper, the skin traders came in to tout for custom. Outside the police were taking up their positions on the moonlit street. The curfew had started and the electricity had been cut off. In a window opposite a fat Afghan, bald without his turban, and stripped to the waist, sat at an upper window smoking opium and gazing at the moon. The last doors were slammed and barred, the policemen went home, and so did the skin traders who seemed to have a special licence to be out late, the moon went in, and even the opium smoker lay back and slept.

Everywhere we went next day in Herat there were three smells. Sweet opium, sour hash and joss sticks. The hash was sold in cakes for four or five shillings, most stall-keepers had a supply they were prepared to part with for the right price, and they regarded the drug as an indulgence they had little use for during business hours. Occasionally at the back of a shop an opium addict, lost in an uncritical torpor, would be tended by his friends; but considering the opportunities they had, the Afghanis could not be claimed as great drug en-

thusiasts. Their visitors, on the other hand, consumed it vora-
ciously. Herat was the first town on the road from Europe
where the rumours came true, the first wet state in the desert
of prohibition.

Herat is the westernmost town in Afghanistan. The centre
of the country is mountainous and sparsely inhabited. Most
of the people live on the fringe plains, and the four big towns,
Kabul in the east, Kandahar in the south, Mazar-i-Sharif in
the north and Herat in the west are linked by one circular
road. All the country's overland trade with the west passes
through Herat. Camel trains from the central region still
limp in carrying skins and carpets and semi-precious stones.
There are skin shops in every street, the bazaar runs the entire breadth of the town, and everywhere the talk is of price.

The old ladies of thirty-five, crouched in the dust, with their
modesty protected by the tattered silk robes which fell from
their head to their feet, leaving only a fretwork visor in front
of their face to let them breathe and see, would stretch out
skinny fingers to suggest – a price. The young men in the
skin shops trying on each other's hats, testing the quality of
each other's cloth continually estimated – the price. If one
was wearing a pair of strong jeans their 'price' was immediately discussed, and it was futile to suggest that they might not
be for sale. Of course, as everyone was well aware, they were
not for sale; that was understood. But surely one could still
carry on a civilised conversation about their value to their
makers, their owners, the assembled company and the uncle
who had expired last year? Everything, whether for sale or
not, had a price.

Herat is more like Baghdad under the Caliph Haroun Al-
Raschid than one has a right to hope that any town will be.
The bazaar was the richest since Istanbul, better by far than
that in Teheran. It was not a covered market, but consisted of
one very long and narrow street where the tall shuttered shops

gave straight on to the unpaved road. As usual it was arranged in order of merchandise, so that the silver merchants were succeeded by the cloth merchants and the cloth merchants by the rope merchants, and the rope merchants by the carpet merchants, and they by the silk merchants who gave way to the vendors of precious and semi-precious stones. These sold rubies and sapphires and turquoise, and jade and agate and lapis lazuli. In the skin shops one could buy fox-throat rugs and lynx hats, leopard skins and bear skins. There were bracelets of silver so heavy that one could not wear them for more than half-an-hour, but the intricate *ménage à trois* with which they were carved might add a third to their value if the right westerner chanced along.

Business in these emporia was a leisurely affair, conducted with gestures over cups of chay and a cannabis pipe, and it was seldom that one could make a fair purchase in less than an hour. The merchants were anxious to seize on their customer's ignorance of local values and to make their first price even higher than usual. Their customers attempted to confuse them into honesty. There were some epic encounters.

On his first day Rat trotted out into the street and put his nose into the breeze and decided that he would be unable to resist the pleasures of the bazaar. He took the precaution before entering it of attaching himself to a dour, muscular man called Fitzroy. Fitzroy had been to Aberdeen University and worked on the trawlers as a cook and hitched to Australia where he had held a very temporary job as a sceneshifter in a television studio. Then he had gone to Israel and got mixed up with the Six-Day War, where he was vividly remembered for an attempt to machine-gun some Druse arab mercenaries on the Israeli side. He was asked to leave and had moved to Nepal, and now he was returning home overland because there had been no British ships in Bombay to work a passage on. For a time he had had no money and nothing to eat except fruit cake. Then in Kabul some mysterious dealings with the international student card syndicate had left him a rich man, and the possessor of a forged student card which gave the name of the Dean of Studies at Aberdeen University as Dupont. Fitzroy was obviously the man to guide Rat round the bazaar and to teach him a little technique.

Together they looked at silver fox furs big enough to cover a double bed (for twelve pounds), and strong leather sandals for fifteen shillings. Rat had himself measured for a blue linen pyjama suit made in the local style for seventeen-and-sixpence and Fitzroy allowed himself to be persuaded into two white silk kaftans for less than five pounds. The best leopard skin in the bazaar only cost thirty pounds but they did not feel like a leopard skin that morning. Fitzroy always made his resources a complete mystery to the merchants and they never knew whether he was one of those westerners without the money to buy himself food or one of those with enough cash in his hip pocket to buy a small lorry.

In the matter of price, although the goods were already extremely cheap, Fitzroy took a certain professional pride in securing the greatest possible reduction. Confusion remained his chief tactic. He would examine every carpet in the courtyard and never do more than ask their price. His first offer was usually too low to suggest serious interest, and since he had time on his hands he might repeat his performance over a number of days, testing the merchant's patience beyond endurance. Above all he never really believed that the bargaining was more than a pleasant way of consuming time, a game perfected for the pleasure of these townsmen. His enthusiasm for the proceedings was therefore strengthened by a sceptical energy which was often too much for the merchant's obstinacy. Only one merchant thoroughly mastered Rat and Fitzroy in this matter of striking a bargain. His name was Aziz Ahmet, a little wizened fellow of twenty-one, with a childhood burn scar making one clear patch on his stubbly cheek; he had his own skin shop just beside the Behzad Hotel, and he rated as the most successful water-boy in town.

Aziz despised cannabis and prayed to God to keep him from it: he never smoked tobacco or touched alcohol or took opium. The travellers would tell him that this was the reason why he looked twice his age, but he would reply scornfully that it was on account of his harder life. He was usually to be seen in the hotel or in front of his shop wearing a brown silk turban wrapped loosely round a skullcap and a nondescript broad-loomed pyjama suit, flashing his perfect white teeth in a welcoming smile. Like his shops his teeth were a mark of his success, though where he had found a pair to fit him so well was a mystery. Above all Aziz's first price was his last, and this was the reason for his commercial prominence in a town whose whole economy was based on barter.

His two skin shops had only the best skins and he also owned a curio shop that traded in guns and trinkets. He was up before anyone else and at eleven he would lunch off sour yogurt and cucumbers which made him belch foully. This was followed by two hours of sleep on the rugs at the back; in addition he prayed five times a day; otherwise he was in business. The skin shops were usually in the hands of his assistants, but he ran the curio shop by himself. His chief worry was that a stoned customer might shoot himself when his back was turned, for among the pieces of mosaic from the wall of the mosque and the metal trinkets, there were some valuable loaded muskets, and it was no good locking the weapons away. They were a lure and an indispensable part of Aziz's business. It had to be possible for the children to shoot themselves – that was the point of the shop.

In Herat boys who wanted to earn some money could always find work as water-carriers; they were paid about one-and-six a day and most of them started before they left school. It was

the ambition of every ambitious child to earn enough money
to buy himself a rich wife. The most valuable girl in town was
the Mayor's daughter, whose hand cost nearly £1,000, and
no woman of esteem was going for less than £250. Clearly
how to save this on one-and-six a day presented a problem.
Aziz had set about solving it.

When he was eight he graduated from water-boy to sewing-
boy in an obscure skin shop at the back of the bazaar. He had
also taken to hanging around the various lodging houses in the
main street in the hope of earning a little money as a guide to
the occasional foreigner who passed through. In this way he
had begun to learn English, and by the time he was fifteen he
had taught himself to speak it well and had also picked up a
little French and German. This made him one of the best
linguists available, for Herat was far from Afghanistan's eastern and southern frontiers which adjoined India and thus far
from the tradition of foreigners.

At fifteen Aziz was a fair businessman and an invaluable
prop to his employer. He was responsible for bringing many
travellers down to the shop at the back of the bazaar, and all
negotiations had to be conducted through him. And then
when the overlanders started to pass through Herat in great
numbers Aziz prevailed on his employer to take a revolution-
ary step; to move his shop out of the bazaar and up to the main
street beside the hotels. Here business could be put on a
different footing altogether. His employer was a shrewd skin
trader who was eager for the increased profits which Aziz
promised him, but he was a simple man and fearful of the
consequences of failure. He felt terribly exposed without the
protective surroundings of the bazaar and he was unable to
speak a word of his new customers' language. Before long Aziz
had persuaded him that they should form a partnership, and
so guarantee his own continuing interest in the shop.

Thus it was that the ex-water-boy turned skin-sewer went

into partnership with his employer and opened up a new shop beside the Behzad Hotel. Within sat the senior partner, cross-legged and sewing skins all day. Without his junior spent the time with his feet up drinking endless cups of tea and gossiping with travellers. It was a just division of labour and theirs quickly became one of the town's most profitable businesses. Within two years other shops had opened up all down the street, each with its bizarre partnership of elderly skin-sewer and multilingual water-boy. In reply Aziz opened his next two shops and abandoned the habit of bargaining over the price of his goods.

It had been a long slow business involving the mastery of a new language, the persuasion of an obstinate and timid employer, and the satisfaction of a fickle and demanding race of customers. But Aziz had won. His first price was his last.

At lunchtime the schoolgirls, aged five to fourteen, would walk back through the streets in their black and white pinafores and every shop front would be crowded with the unmarried men of Herat, young and old, eager to inspect the only unveiled women they might see that day. Aziz could look them over as well now, balancing beauty and price and making himself promises. He too could pick and choose, his fantasies richly shot with fact.

The days passed pleasantly. Herat was a small town and it did not take long to establish a regular acquaintance, to know at which doors one would be greeted and pressed to chay or a smoke, and to map one's route accordingly. Sometimes we saw big Jake, but he only glowered at us, and after a while he forgot to do even that. One morning when Rat was walking on the edge of town he was overcome by the heat and was forced to rest at the side of a deserted road. To his horror the only person in sight was Jake who loomed towards him, shimmering through the haze, his long nightgown flapping purposefully round his mighty feet. He approached and passed disdainfully by. It was his version of the parable of the Good Samaritan.

A usual day's work in Herat was the cashing of travellers' cheques. This meant an expedition to the banks which were clustered defensively in the southern part of the town, and were all equipped with tiny aged guards who stood beneath the fruit trees outside armed with rusty shot guns. The rifles were invariably taller than the guards, and nobody liked to ask precisely how they had come by these ancient British weapons.

When you had passed the guards and found a promising room in the bank, you were faced with six or seven men sitting behind enormous red topped desks; and whichever man you approached would gesticulate irritably to one of his colleagues. Finally one would enquire your business and then, after another long silence while his quill pen scratched across the fibrous brown bill paper, too rough and absorbent to reproduce anything more than a series of blotches, he would ask how much you wanted to cash. The only way to speed up this process was to break off negotiations and irritate the guard, either by asking to fire his gun or, more resourcefully, by suggesting that he pose for a picture. In the latter case he would be pounced on instantly by two bank messengers and posed in any number of positions, full face, profile, arms sloped, smiling, looking fierce, until he would tire and insist that we be attended to at once, and we would leave him struggling with his tormentors, like the jury lizard in *Alice*, for the right to adopt his preferred physical attitude.

The interview secured, the real bargaining of the day began. Where were the travellers' cheques? Which bank? Never heard of it. Hasty glance through official international specimen book, reassuringly stamped with the familiar names of all the British banks. Can't see your cheque here. It would be pointed out. Painfully close scrutiny of the dummy and comparison of the proffered cheque. No. Your cheque is a forgery. Look, the official one in the book has this word prominently overprinted in red. SPECIMEN. Your cheque lacks this. So sorry.

Hysterical scenes. Quite useless. Without the magic word on our cheques there would be no chance of an exchange of Afghanis.

Did the demented fool realise that without glittering afghanis we were in danger of becoming a burden on the state? Did he, did he?

Nonsense; there was always the independent Pashtani bank, or even the black market. Be off with us and our dud cheques.

So we would trek miserably across town to a private bank where, after another long delay, a clerk might be reckless enough to overlook the absence of the word 'specimen' on our cheques – for a lower rate of exchange of course. Once, infuriated with these delays, we indulged in a long ritual of insults, invoking the King, the Cabinet, the President of the Bank, the clerk before us and any other customers in earshot. Instead of hauling us off for a well-deserved gaol sentence the clerk became emotionally wrought, and immediately offered to take our cheques to the black market himself in order to find a better rate of exchange. In a moment he was out of the first floor window and down a fruit tree that stood outside and within ten minutes he was back with the loot. Everyone was delighted with this initiative except Rat, who told him it was the most ridiculous thing he had ever heard of. The clerk looked hurt.

Not all the travellers who picked their way to Herat were westerners. One voluble party of millionaire anti-imperialists from Pakistan drove in, their carefully-laid plans to fly to Rome foxed by the cholera restrictions. It seemed to them that the quickest way to get to Teheran was to bribe a frontier guard, and so they had hired a car in Kabul and been driven to Herat in preparation. Somehow this plan always failed: the bribe was not enough, or there was too much moonlight, or an inspecting officer was in the area. Several times they slipped out after curfew only to be back in the hotel next morning. Once they disappeared altogether in the direction of Kandahar with rumours of a private aeroplane, but even then they came back to plot rearrangements and refinements and strategies in the hall of the Behzad. In the intervals between these forays they would harangue any Englishmen within hearing on the woes of Empire and the evils of the fair haired ones. They were eloquent men, and the star rubies on their fingers glittered as they emphasised a point about colonial exploitation.

At first we stayed in Herat because we had arrived somewhere. Then we stayed there because the Americans had promised us a lift and they had just a few more furs to buy. Then we stayed on because we liked it so much.

The Americans liked it too. Joe was on the run from the draft and was grateful for the lack of interest. He believed in spending every day like there'd be no tomorrow, and it was he who challenged Fitzroy to a horse carriage race down the main street. Joe had become friendly with one of the drivers and spent hours helping him to polish his car and feed his horse. They did not talk much, but the driver was delighted with his new friend, a man who clearly appreciated a well-polished carriage with brass wishbones and a silk canopy, and he was happy to be of service to so gilded a traveller.

The 'service' turned out to be the horse carriage race which Fitzroy won at disappointingly less than a canter, since Joe's car got caught up in a crowd which had gathered to see a snake which one of the water boys had scooped from the gutter at the side of the road. Joe's challenge died somewhere in the crowd to a chorus of Afghani curses and muffled cries of 'move, mother-fuckers, move'.

The girls meanwhile embarked on a massive spending spree. They bought silk dresses and trousers, and beads and rings and bracelets. They spent most of the day bargaining and would return to the five o'clock cannabis parties to show off their wares and to plan any additional embroidering. One could not pass the fur shops without seeing one or other resplendent in a hat or a coat or a rug, drooping like narcissi in front of the glass, and absently disputing the price.

One dusk the quiet was shattered with loud cries and bangs. Everyone rushed to the door expecting a raid by hill bandits or at least the long-awaited rising by dissident police. But it turned out to be one of our buccaneers, shouting and cursing outside the shuttered door of the tailor's shop, enraged by the tightness under the arm of one of his shirts and anxious to discuss the matter with the proprietor. Another small crowd gathered and two policemen watched him uninterestedly. They only began to move in his direction when the kicks from his Texan boots started to shake the whole front of the shop. Before they could get there Aziz had led him away with promises of a terrible retribution in the morning.

In the evening we would sit with Aziz and listen to the merchant talking of his ancestors and boasting what warriors they were. Most of his boasting was true. Only a few years before an eccentric Russian hotelier had been ferrying a luxury caravan across the southern part of the country and had been attacked one night in traditional style by the local inhabitants. They were called bandits, but they were no more bandits than Aziz. They were just the villagers of the area who had smelt booty on the evening breeze.

Already Herat is marked by a piecemeal modernity. Electricity is now supplied, though only during the evening, and it is cut off at midnight. In some buildings there are rusted water cisterns which work when an old man is toiling at the hand-pump below. From the back windows of the hotel we could see the more traditional way of dealing with the matter. People would spend all day wandering apparently aimlessly round a lunar range of low mounds and fetid ponds. Occasionally they would halt and crouch and then depart. The random contours of this area were no freak of nature but the result of a process of accretion through the centuries where men had been alternately preoccupied with the need for privacy and the means of constructing it. The hens which provided our chicken and egg kebabs scratched happily around on the dung heap.

Herat had several chemist's shops, each with a sticker for Sandoz (the makers of L.S.D.) in the window, each stocked solely with antibiotics and vitamin pills. We never saw an Afghani enter one, which was not surprising since the cheapest vitamins cost fivepence a tablet and it was doubtful if most of the inhabitants could afford a month's supply in a year. One shopkeeper, a cousin of Aziz, had three wives and thirty-two children, fourteen of whom were still alive. But the survivors of this high mortality rate showed the legendary hill toughness. In contrast to both Persia and Pakistan there were no beggars in Herat, and few cripples, although the scars of small-pox and impetigo were on many faces.

The most immediate effect of the overlanders on the local economy was an increase in the fur price. There must have been ten or a dozen skin shops each with two or three good leopard skins, usually able to sell one a week. How long this could continue was not a question which had yet occurred to the hunters, although they were already complaining that the animals were not as plentiful as they had been. There were no licences needed to kill the leopards or bears or foxes that were now being so determinedly pursued, and if it continues unchecked, the demand will certainly exterminate the supply.

When they become aware of this problem, the Afghanis will treat it with the same watchful detachment that they apply to most aspects of life. For though one never doubted one's welcome among them, it was clear that their hospitality was tempered with caution. For them, the overlanders were a new phenomenon, a race of visiting foreigners who did not apparently arrive with any imperial intentions and so did not necessarily require the traditional bloodthirsty response. But they gave the impression of waiting until you had passed some test before they admitted you to their full confidence. They were hard men in a hard country. Travelling halfway across the world without money or transport was well enough in its way, but it remained a diversion from the serious business of surviving in Afghanistan and they wanted evidence of competence at this before committing themselves to friendship.

There may have been other reasons for the unnerving feeling of being watched. It may have been no more than a reflection of the Pathan's traditional reserve about hospitality – the rule that so long as you were their guest no harm should come to you, but that as soon as you had left the house you were fair game. It was an attitude that added a certain flavour to their entertaining. One departed with a new insight into the predicament of the fatted calf.

We decided to leave Herat because eventually the Americans bought so many clothes that they had to sell their van. It was a sad moment when that temple passed into other and less appreciative hands and our companions were turned out on to the road, and like the rest of us became vulnerable to the mischances of other people's journeys. Until then they had travelled well, they smelt clean, they ate well, they always had somewhere to sleep, they could come and go as they pleased. With cannabis and antibiotics and Leonard Cohen tapes they had all that life could withhold. The last of the stores had to be consumed and so we shared a feast with them when the cooks were double stoned and, in anticipation of many hundreds of miles of egg kebab, we gorged ourselves on rice and black bean soup followed by a drink of chocolate fudge, rum fudge, powdered milk and cocoa. Disgusting, but delicious.

After the Americans had sold the van there was nothing to keep us in Herat, no more excuses we could reasonably make.

One night, just before we left, Rat was returning to the hotel when he saw some new arrivals who seemed familiar; it was Barry and Ann. So far from being days ahead of us on the road they had been days behind. They had been staying with a chemist in the north of town, Ann, as usual, guaranteeing a special interest among the local people in their party's comfort. We were all invited to supper with the chemist. We drove out through the dark streets in a horse carriage beyond the flickering safety of the dim street lamps. Nothing moved except the night breeze, until a dog rushed at the horse, causing it to shy. After a while the path became too bad for the carriage to continue. We got out, rather reluctantly remembering the dog, and continued down a narrow lane on foot, following the driver's vague gesture towards a lamp flickering at the end of the lane.

It was warm and we were to eat outside, on the verandah of a half-built house surrounded by a high walled garden at this moment filled with corn. The servant with the lamp took us in through a low arch and beckoned us to sit on some carpets. Then he left to get the food and there was no light except the stars and no sound except the mice and the wind in the grass. Our host disappeared and reappeared apologetically throughout the meal. He explained that he would rather have entertained us at home but that there were difficulties about his wife unveiling, and he was forced to carry the food across the road through the darkness and serve us in the garden. It seemed an unlikely story. He showed us round the skeleton house and took us up to the incomplete top floor. Up there, under the sky, we were above the shelter of the wall and the wind blew harder and from the direction of the scented orchards. Our host served a heavy spicy tea and warned us not to move far while he was gone, for fear of snakes. He left us a lamp whose dim circle of light only emphasised the surrounding gloom. Somewhere beyond its pool something moved, a man coughed, and the sky darkened.

At this point Rat decided that the tea had been drugged and that the whole occasion was a carefully staged trick to rape him. Why was the food so cold if it had only been brought from the house across the lane? We were trapped here with only a dying lamp in a garden infested with snakes, mad dogs beyond the walls and the nearest help perhaps a mile away through the darkness and up wind. Convinced for some reason that it was he who was at risk rather than Ann, Rat rushed off into the night and left the rest of us to pick our way through the grass to the gate and there surprise our host whispering with a watchman beneath the arch.

So the party ended abruptly and we never discovered whether Rat's suspicions were justified. In any event we were escorted back to the edge of town by the chemist who, before he left us, had one last request.

'Please tell no one you have supper with Afghani. Afghani very bad. He very jealous.' He pressed our hands warmly and disappeared into the dark. The supper party remained a mystery.

On the next morning, the twelfth of June, we decided to leave. Herat had been the best place yet but it was not the end of the journey, and it was almost becoming difficult to plan our departure. Our friends there were caught in a different time scale to those who passed through their town. We were travelling slowly and thoroughly through distant places by choice, and just because we believed that this was the best way to travel we were to some extent indulging ourselves. But they were rooted like the fly in amber to this one time and place – Herat, now. Even Kabul, the capital of their country and only twenty-four hours away by road, was further than most of them were ever likely to go. These men would live and die where they had been born, like their fathers and grandfathers before them, and as far as they could see, their children to follow, pinned between two great wildernesses, and suffering such intermittent contact with others of their race as chance secured for them.

We said goodbye to Aziz and gave him a tin of D.D.T. which was unobtainable locally and for which he thanked us. He was only puzzled that it was a gift, since it seemed too insignificant a thing to demand much gratitude and we were now all deprived of the pleasure of arguing about its price.

Above my bed somebody had scrawled 'hic sum sed hic non mano'. It was the only enduring effect any of its occupants had had on that bug-ridden room. We packed up, underpaid the hotel owner, who was insisting that we owed him for more egg kebabs than any sane man could have consumed in a year, and, to the boom of the midday cannon, clambered aboard the overnight bus for Kabul.

At first sight, the bus was very far from comfortable. It was cramped, without cushions, and there was a most curious passenger directly in front of us: a short man, with a bald moon face which hung from the edge of his grubby turban like an oil globule, and in the inner sleekness of which was caught a most foolish smile. He kneeled on the bench in front and just beamed, and it was not comfortable at all. Rat had the window seat and became exhilarated at the wild, shouted prayer of our shotgun guard, who leapt on to the stern ladder as we drew out of the compound. He was dressed in black, both turban and gown, and as he was now hunched into the wind on the roof of the bus, we could see his shadow in the speeding dust by the side of the road, occasionally beating a wild tattoo on the tin luggage. Armed with a brutish-looking weapon, he was a certain asset, to Rat's way of thinking. He was setting the journey's style.

As the bus moved off down the main street, past the Behzad, whose proprietor was shaking his head sorrowfully, another reason for discomfiture became apparent. For we were not alone; not isolated among the Afghanis. Just across the gangway, sullen and equally suspicious, were two more overlanders. One was stopped and rather owl-like in his thick-rimmed glasses, the other shorter and more muscular and in a most curious salmon-pink string vest. For some time we ignored each other, determined not to let the coincidence of our shared and remote journey become an excuse for conversation. Then, after perhaps half an hour, our mood changed with a need for water, and the suspicion gave way to the beginnings of the usual comradeship.

They were on their way to Australia and had been travelling for over a year. Roger, the shorter one in the string vest, had suffered from amœbic dysentery for most of the time, and three English hospitals had failed to cure a germ he had picked up in Kuwait. Now they were on the road again after a six-month delay in Istanbul where they too had become involved with a European smuggling racket.

We left Herat by the road to Kandahar, a town which would mark the southernmost point of our journey, and which was by all accounts already wickedly hot. The road had been built by the Russians some years before. It was certainly an improvement on the dust tracks to the west, being made of successive concrete slabs joined by ridges of cement. This gave our journey a syncopated accompaniment which after a while sank like the ticking of a clock into the unconscious depths of the mind. It was a rough apology for a highway, but it would last for ever without need of surface repair. Its orderly ticking reminded us that we were finished with wildernesses, we were returning to another civilisation.

Outside the day burnt on. We were still in a dust desert but now there was the occasional broad dry river bed and abrupt sugar-loaf mountains. They stood quite alone, and rose immediately to several thousand feet, and were never linked by a chain. There seemed to be no reason why that particular part of the earth should have chosen to rise so immodestly above its surroundings.

When the bus halted the atmosphere inside it became stifling, a change which the native passengers bore with noticeably more composure than the overlanders. They lolled on their benches in the heat. Three of them were evidently of some importance since they had been seen off by their sons, two army officers and several servants. The servants had called down blessings on their journey and had been showered with coins. Their masters were tall men, straight and fierce, in splendid silk turbans with dark eyes and white teeth, only slightly unshaven. They had a patrician air, and one in startling contrast, had blue eyes. It was said that Afghanis with blue eyes were descended from the soldiers of Sikander of Macedon, son of the Barbarian, Alexander the Great. The patricians had exactly the faces of the colonels and explorers and minor viceroys who had once held their neighbours in the weak net of empire. The sort of English faces one sees in the expensive parts of a race meeting or beneath a wedding marquee, wearing the only ceremonial uniform left to them, the morning coat. In Afghanistan they are still the faces of confident men, accustomed to use their fellows, who find it a pleasant way to live.

Towards mid-afternoon Moonface began to torment us so much that we decided something must be done. Friendly suggestions that he beam elsewhere in the bus had the opposite effect to that intended: the idiot orb merely loomed closer, even to within six inches of the Rat's own face. The patricians had by this time noted the discomfiture of the foreigners, and with archetypal detachment settled down to enjoy the sight. Here was a nuisance offered to some strangers. How would they get round it?

Rat tentatively pushed the globe away. Bad move. It beamed yet wider and seemed to be organising itself for an embrace. The moment had come for action. Rat banged his steel water bottle hard on to Moonface's hands, wrapped round the bar between them, and then shoved him backwards as hard as he could. A cry, and the great moon sank from sight on to the floor, there to roll around in loud agony. Decisive enough, but what would the three patricians do to retrieve the lost dignity of their injured idiot countryman? The idiot himself settled the matter. The howls of pain suddenly stopped, to be replaced by floods of tears. It was crying. Bursts of laughter all round the bus. Amused spittings on the floor. The globe sobbed himself to sleep, and we too could relax.

Spitting was a feature of this journey: the men would take some green powder from a tin and start to chew it. It looked like grass shavings, but it tasted hot and had a mildly intoxicating effect. When they had chewed the powder out of the shavings the passengers spat a green cud on to the floor, which was encrusted like a cow shed. It seemed to soothe travel sickness.

Beside Moonface sat an ancient Afghan who was travelling alone and who insisted on keeping the window wide open. Throughout the journey he vomited and hacked and suffered violent fits. He wept soundlessly to himself, and at one point seemed about to expire. Here, unfortunately, he failed, and he continued to drench me in the secretions of his various ducts and orifices all the way to Kandahar. Wonderful that so ancient and dry a husk could flow with that much sap.

E

Towards evening we passed a mirage. Beside the road there appeared a spotless modern building as out of place in that wilderness as a mud fort in Whitehall. It was a prestige hotel built by the Russians at the same time as the road. It had air conditioning, a swimming pool, a kitchen that could feed 400 and, whisper it, European lavatories. However it was empty. There were no guests, there had never been any guests, and so there was no chef and the cooking was done in a shack at the back. We stopped in front of it and bought some yogurt and cucumber from a nomad. The cucumber made a welcome change from the luke-warm brown fluid that was all that remained in our water bottles. We ate it all, and used the husk as a tooth-pick.

At sundown the bus stopped again and everyone got out to pray. They stalked away from us into the desert, spreading out over many hundreds of yards, and we climbed on to the roof to inspect them. It was a cool evening, and they faced the western sunset and Mecca, dotted across a plateau that ran from the road to a parallel river bed, all with their backs to us, standing or kneeling, some walking until they were almost lost to sight. One set up a thin wail. There was no urgency in their movements; they strolled with linked arms in their white robes for half a mile or so to address their God, and then they strolled back again. Nothing lived in the devastation around them. Only the sun moved. On the roof of the bus the overlanders watched them in silence.

Night came, with the mountains like beasts closing in on either side of our seemingly tiny car, and an incredible multitude of stars, red and blue and green, opening out overhead. It became clear why astrology had originated in the east. At some point we stopped beside a hut for a meal. There were no lamps, only a fire; and in the blackness a plate with something warm on it was placed before us. Some said it had been a goat. Others, a dog. It tasted quite good.

We reached Kandahar just after dawn. The bus drew into an enormous courtyard, filled at this hour with legions of empty buses. In the shade of the early sunshine it was freezing, but in the pale light at the compound's western edge the heat already hung heavy. We pushed among a group of porters and shared their tea and bread, and waited for the next stage to Kabul.

But before we could leave on the bus a battle had to be waged for the right to board it. Three were due to leave at the same time; one was a plush new German luxury coach, another a less comfortable standard version of the same, and then a third arrived from Herat which was truly appalling. It disgorged two Canadians with a strong story to tell about a flock of sheep on the seat in front. They had started the journey in laundered white shirts and fresh jeans, and looking at them we could see their point.

It accordingly became the stated intention of the six overlanders now assembled to board the luxury coach. Equally it became the declared intention of the officials to ensure that the riff-raff from the west board the sheep waggon. A mighty clamour arose in the early morning calm. Luggage was piled and unpiled from one coach roof after another. Porters rushed from bus to bus, the harassed ticket collector ordered, suggested, entreated. Advance parties boarded and were ejected from the cool interior of the big German job. It seemed most likely that we should miss all three buses. Finally the Rat organised a diversion. A combined frontal assault was launched on the luxury coach while Rat crept to the back door of the medium-standard one and overwhelmed the startled old man on the cross bench. The frontal assault was then relinquished and we all piled in behind him. We waited until the porters had been diverted to other business and then loaded up our luggage. We were off.

In the desert going north to Kabul from Kandahar there is

a multiplicity of earthen forts. They are continually being vacated and replaced by others of slightly more sophisticated design. There is never any question of altering them, it seems cheaper just to throw up another a few hundred yards away. But those occupied are defended with a serious military purpose, evidently in anticipation of a war fought without artillery or aircraft. The abandoned ones are allowed to crumble into the dust from which they were originally scraped. Like the dead villages in Persia there was little trace of the part they had once played in the affairs of the region. They simply resumed their former status, indistinguishable from the dust they had sprung from.

Every hour or so the bus stopped at a road block set up by the health officials. It seemed that all those travelling east had to be vaccinated against cholera. We carried vaccination certificates stamped impressively with the name and sign of the World Health Organisation, but these forms were not enough to satisfy the soldiers who boarded the bus. At every stop they wished to ensure that we accompany them to their dark huts, there to receive another injection. The likely effect was a dose of hepatitis, rather than protection from cholera, and so we resisted the medical orderlies with all our strength and were aided in this by the other passengers who only wanted to finish their journey. The soldiers, fortunately, were not trusted with any weapons other than spades and after a while the driver crashed the monotonous barricades.

We had been promised that we would reach Kabul that day, and gradually after hours of desert the countryside began to change its character. It grew greener, the frequent water conduits appeared to be having some effect, and though the land remained savage and unwelcoming we started to climb a little and the variety thus achieved was a relief. Finally we rounded a bend and could see on the horizon the plateaued capital of Afghanistan, a dusty city perched on barren hills.

As we approached the town, fruit bearers and flocks of animals crowded the smart American road. We passed a stream and in the middle of it, on its back, lay a dead donkey. It had swollen to the size of a water buffalo, and five rigid legs towered above it like a crown. On closer inspection the fifth limb proved to be the swiftest way of establishing its sex. A little further downstream a man was washing fruit.

The bus was unloaded in Kabul by porters in rope and sacking who squabbled incessantly about who was to unload which bag and at what cost. Roger short-circuited the process by unloading all our stuff himself. Then a dapper man who spoke English with a German accent approached and offered round his card. It said, 'Sina Hotel. *New, Clean and Satisfactory Services. Location Share Nau, Kabul, Afghanistan save parking, and green garden*', and looked rather too good to be true. 'A special feature,' he murmured to those who looked doubtful. 'Separate bedside lockers.' The Canadians decided that this was a hassle and wandered off in search of the famous Noor. The German gentleman offered the rest of us free taxis to his place, and we accepted promptly. It proved to be cheaper than the famous Noor.

In the Sina we slept in one big room and had breakfast in the garden under a fruit tree and tried to beat the wasps off the jam. For variety there was an air-conditioned cafe at the end of town which sold buffalo steaks and apple pie and iced coca-cola, and it must be admitted that many of those making the great trek into a primitive past sullied their record here in gross fashion by gorging themselves on the decadent tasties. It was called the Khyber Restaurant.

Sitting there one night we were approached by an Afghani who spoke good English and who explained that on the next day his mother was to have an operation for a serious heart condition. Before the operation could be carried out many pints of blood were needed; this blood was rare among

Afghanis, less so among westerners, could we help him? The Rat enquired if he was paying for this blood and the man looked rather shocked and confirmed that he was. The Rat said that he was not selling any of *his* blood, perhaps some of the westerners at other tables might be. The Afghani rose and said, 'On behalf of the lady I am thanking you gentlemen for your patience,' and left. His exaggerated courtesy made no impression at all on Rat who was quite clear about how to deal with local vampires with designs on his vital bodily fluids.

Kabul was a route centre. From here you could travel north to the Hindu Kush, or Mazar-i-Sharif, where the buccaneers had heard tales about packs of wild Afghani hounds, and unconfirmed stories of camel polo played with a sheep's carcase for a ball; or you could go south to Goa, or north-east to Kashmir; or just opt out of the journey altogether and for forty pounds make your way via Tashkent and Leningrad to a Baltic port and thence to Aberdeen. Peace River John, intending to do this had flown to Tashkent where he had been given three years in a labour camp for possessing cannabis; it had not been quite the short cut he had hoped for.

Kabul was also the last place on the road for Karakul coats, and the only place for lapis lazuli. The lapis came down from the hills and was an invaluable investment since its value rose as soon as it left the country. To the west they preferred its blue qualities, the more blues it held the better; to the east, and especially in India, the customers were more interested in its golden possibilities, the more sullied it was with dull yellow threads, the more the Indians would pay for it. In the stone shops near the police station one could spend many happy hours bargaining for lumps of uncut or unpolished lapis.

In one shop there was a determined little boy whose task it was to fondle the customer's hands. If dissuaded he adopted a most professional 'hell hath no fury' expression, but usually started up again within a minute or so. God knows what an

English juvenile court would have made of him; God knows what he would have done to the officers of the court. Halfway through one performance Perkins came in.

'Aah,' said the little fellow's father. 'He your friend?'

'Yes.'

'Aaaahh.'

'No, no. He's just my friend. Not my *friend*.'

'Ah.' And the little boy was deployed to try his luck with Perkins.

The centre of the overland community was the Noor. A notice on the wall there said, 'Smoking of Hashish is now being forbidden on or in the premises of the Noor Hotel. The Management.' In fact The Management, an affable cannabis enthusiast, was usually to be seen in the garden smoking with his guests and one or two off-duty policemen. The smell of the weed, as it drifted through the vegetable leaves and over the recumbent disciples, was everywhere. The purpose of the notice was obscure.

Not all the guests at the Noor were pukka drop outs. Two slight girls from Taiwan, whose journey was a mirror of ours, since they were striving for the west and California, arrived bearing enormous rucksacks. In the garden they would exercise among the cannabis sleepers with skipping ropes – and medicine balls.

The day before we left there were two French arrivals in town. They wore loose turbans and woollen night gowns in the local manner. Beneath the gowns protruded inelegant gym shoes. The hotel dogs never got used to their turbans, and whenever they moved out of their rooms into the garden the air grew thick with snarling and French oaths.

The buccaneers did not reach Kabul before we left; neither did Barry and Ann, who had set out to travel there slowly with the chemist and some of his friends. We left Rat and got a lift through Pakistan to Amritsar just over the Indian border. As soon as we descended from the hills the heat closed in like a kiln. Here there was the Golden Temple of Amritsar, the holiest place in the Sikh religion. It was night time, we removed our shoes and covered our heads and went in. The marble on the floor burnt our feet. There were high walls and a central courtyard, and in the centre of this a dark lake round which the children played, and in the centre of that a delicate temple. Everywhere the noise of the singing from the temple boomed eerily through the darkness – amplified by a primitive electrical system. To reach the Temple you had to cross a flagged stone bridge. There were priests there and a band and the sacred book. They offered us a sweet yellow paste which it was impossible to consume and impossible to throw away. It grew hot in our hands and stained our clothing. By the steps which led down from the four gates of the temple into the court there was a cluster of beggars and mystics, asleep on the warm, warm floor. We spent the night in a miserable rooming house on the other side of town unable to sleep for more than a few minutes. Every hour or so we took a shower from the lukewarm water tank and returned to bed without drying, and so gained ten minutes relief. There was a broken electric fan on the roof, and wicker screens to exclude the cockroaches and the heat. Both slipped past it with ease. When we left in the morning a fellow guest, an intrepid lady with one eye from the mid-western United States, slipped a card into our hands.

'This'll come in handy when you boys have decided to settle,' she murmured. It read, INTERNATIONAL EDUCATION INSTITUTE: UNITED NATIONS PLAZA: NEW YORK CITY N.Y. Her eye as she smiled held a promise of diplomas and wall-to-wall carpets and regular soap. She was a lady who had discovered her life's work.

The air in northern India in the weeks before the monsoon is as tangible as the other elements. It is as hot as fire, as thick as water. It becomes an effort to part it. It burns you and soaks you at the same time. If you step into it from an air-conditioned building, the impression is of a physical blow; the heat rises from the ground and strikes. If you remain still, it enfolds you gently; if you try to move through it, it gains a malignant confidence and seizes you.

A nation which has to occupy itself in such a climate, which has to plan and build and exercise power and observation and change its mind and start again, might well expect to find survival hard. As we approached Delhi along the Ganges there was an impression of a listless people waiting for the rain, on a brown earth, in a grey light, under a thick cloud of yellow dust that blanketed sunlight and shadows alike. And yet, despite this, others worked and planned and built. Somehow the effort was made. Every morning the crowds who swarmed from the shanty towns outside the cities were dressed in fresh white clothes. The officials stood upright in khaki uniforms which had been starched that morning and would be changed at midday. The sahibs had left twenty years before, but signs of their passing were everywhere. In the accents of the customs guards, in the manner in which the soldiers cared for their weapons, in the neat way in which the telegraph wires were joined to their posts. After Afghanistan the contrast was clearly marked. People have survived in this part of the world, and instead of just trying to sleep off the whole experience as a nightmare, have organised for themselves a life-style customarily followed in a temperate climate.

The second impression of India, even in the monochrome weeks before the rain, is one of colour. The colour bleeds out over the land. In the birds and the trees and the river mud there is a luxurious waste of colour. It is as though you are seeing colours for the first time. Suddenly and for no particular reason, the second man in a crowd, the third barrow in a market, blind you with their interior light.

E*

In the Delhi Coffee House the overlanders lay about like beached fish, waiting for the rains to wash them out on to the road again. While they waited they drank iced coffee and swopped the usual poverty stories.

'I met this Peace Corps worker who used to hear a baby crying in one of the huts in his village. Finally he went in and asked what was the matter and found that the baby's eyes were bandaged. Underneath each bandage there was a leech. The parents said they had put them there because the child would one day have to be a beggar, and they wanted him to be a good one, so they were making him as ugly as possible. Isn't that a wild story?'

Among them, but apart, was a man we had heard of as far back as Istanbul. He was a Dane called Eik who had spent seven years on the road and who returned to it again and again. He was as thin as the Indians, with a shaven head and a scarred body, and he had long since abandoned the clothes in which he had set out from home. Instead he wore the rags of a saddhu, an itinerant alms-taker, and carried a staff to help him walk. He found it impossible to wear shoes, a municipal bus in Cambridge having removed three of his toes. His staff also came in handy for discouraging the over-curious children in the Moslem part of the bazaar. Almost alone among the people waiting in Delhi he seemed to have discovered some purpose in his travels. Last year he had returned to Denmark and formed a group and released a record. It had been a success and Eik had left immediately.

Now he was waiting for his friend Hank to be released from jail where he was a 'B' class prisoner serving a three-month sentence for 'forging his passport'. Eik was not too worried about Hank: the 'B' class was apparently the place. You had a servant to wake you with breakfast and there was a garden outside your room. In the 'C' class the prisoners fought each other for blankets and food.

Hank's real offence had not even been in the penal code. One evening he had been hanging around outside the post office when he was approached by a suave young Indian who insisted that he knew a better place to post letters. They drove off in the Indian's car and stopped at an extensive bungalow behind the parliament building.

'This is the house of my uncle,' explained the young man. 'He is the President of the National Rifle Association and,' his voice dropped to a confidential level, 'a very big shot.' Uncle was a Member of Parliament, a crack marksman, and a multi-millionaire. He wanted to see Hank.

The President of the Indian National Rifle Association was fat. He sat crosslegged on a couch in a cool inner room, while his nephew rubbed his rheumatic joints. Hank sat down opposite and the dignified old man fixed a suggestive smile on him. He was the image of jovial corruption. The room was dark and the doors were well guarded, nobody on the road, nobody in the world knew that Hank was sitting here opposite the obscenely creaking Sikh while the air-conditioner roared in the background. The talk wandered; money, accommodation, the heat. Outside the water sprinkled on to just about the only green lawn in Delhi. The subject of Cambridge University came up. Hank claimed to have been at the same college as the Sikh and this cramped the old gentleman's style. It recalled the senator and man of liberal culture and so the old man bade farewell to his guest. His nephew was slipped five shillings for an afternoon's unsuccessful poncing and Hank was driven back into town. A few days later Hank was arrested.

While Eik waited he begged for his food and his cinema tickets. He could beg about fifteen shillings on a good day, five bob on a bad one. It was a considerable income since his lodgings in the old city cost him sixpence a night and in any case he could always sleep out in the open for free, in company with half the city's population.

Before we left Delhi the Indian newspapers opened a long series of investigations into 'the hippy phenomenon.' Startled groups of tattered overlanders were approached in the coffee house and invited to eyeball-to-eyeball confrontations with teams of sleuths from the *Statesman* or the *Times of India*. One such confrontation was organised by a Mr Naqui and it proved to be a small milestone in international misunderstanding.

Mr Naqui felt that this was the time to air a few of the unspoken questions about the appearance of this generation of filthy post-Imperialists in New Delhi, a city which had been constructed by their conquering forefathers. What did this anti-materialist philosophy have to offer India, and what was the connection between these international beggars and the European student revolt?

His visitors knew little of their imperial past, denied any community of interest with the Paris revolution of May 1968 and were bored by questions about how they lived ·without money. There were long pauses while neighbouring reporters pretended to be working and the atmosphere in the air-conditioned office grew strained. Finally discussion got round to girls. Why were there so few among the overlanders? An explanation about the number of attacks followed; the particular dangers of neighbouring Moslem countries were mentioned. Mr Naqui wanted this explained at greater length. 'Well. You know ... Moslems ...' said the spokesman. There was a pause. 'I am a Moslem,' said Mr Naqui. The meeting finished.

Back beneath the white columns of Connaught Circus Eik was being accosted by an old beggar woman who ended by giving him a few pennies. Then she shamed a wealthy Indian who had been buying pigskin luggage into giving Eik a pound. We spent the last evening with Racquel Welch in *One Million Years BC*.

VI A dance in the wind

The Indian trains were flamboyantly unreliable, stifling and hopelessly overcrowded. The third class had a further distinction : it was virtually free. Because of the great numbers travelling it was quite impossible for any ticket collection to take place during the journey, and at the stations most of the mob just rushed the barrier.

Euphoric at the thought of a free ride as far as the Nepalese border we took the wrong train and did not discover our mistake until we reached Patna on the south side of the Ganges. Not only was this too far south; it was too far east as well. We climbed wearily off the train and made enquiries for the Ganges ferry. In Delhi it had been reliably reported that the monsoon had reached Patna some weeks earlier. The men in Delhi should not believe everything they read in the weather reports. Patna lay under the same yellow pall as everywhere else, and the people waited sullenly for the rain.

We found the river with the aid of a bicycle rickshaw boy. There were no buses in town so we succumbed to his blandishments and loaded our packs and ourselves on to his carriage. He carved a path through the milling streets and the solid air ringing his bell furiously – the sinews on his legs standing out before my blurred vision like cords. Even on this short journey we both managed to sleep; free train rides are not restful. At the quay a great crowd was gathered waiting patiently for the boat. By the booking-office window an old lady was sitting in a pool of her own water; a few feet away her grandchildren slept on the floor. Other children played by the river's edge, jumping in and out of the brown flood and occasionally retrieving charred wooden trays that floated downstream, which they raced against each other. They were the cremated remains of the funeral rafts from Benares.

Eventually a tubby paddle steamer with a thin smokestack slipped its moorings and drew in to the quay. There was a great rush to board the single gangplank. Somehow the press forced itself on to the deck and after another pointless delay we set off. Out into the holy Ganges we paddled, while the glutinous tide rushed past the ship, its surface speckled with ashes and garlands; for the first time since the ferry over the Bosphorus we were crossing more than a stream. Nobody could say when we would reach the far shore, or whether there would be a train there. Nothing was visible out on the water except the haze and the rushing ashes. Shortly after sailing we went aground.

The voyage dragged on during the afternoon. Perkins slept heavily sitting on a bench and a curious crowd gathered silently around him to puzzle over the contrast between his ragged shoes and his expensive cameras. Smuts from the smokestack soon covered every passenger. They were less visible on us than on the white-clad Indians. Towards evening the mist cleared a little and we could make out a mud bank on the horizon. Slowly, silently, we approached it – beyond, a rise in the ground revealed a railhead. As the boat drew in fifty men in black shorts and faded red vests, oblivious of the churning blades, leapt on board with a wild shout. They were not dacoits but freelance porters, and gangs of them fought for the privilege of carrying the richer-looking bags. We stumbled ashore and began the ascent to the train. Someone had said that it went to the border.

Even by Indian standards this train was remarkable. For a start it was the most crowded train we had yet seen. It was physically impossible to board it. People were already standing along its outer side, clinging to the window frames and climbing on to its roof. There was no question of us *and* our packs getting a ride. One or the other had to go. Nor were we the only disappointed travellers. Struggling up the hill behind us came a litter carried by two porters. A girl lay inside it, thin and pouring with sweat. At every lurch she cried out in pain; she was followed by her family, her mother comforting her, the rest silent. There was apparently no room for her either.

Following the litter to the front, we found a solution. There was a first-class truck which was virtually empty. The girl in the litter was lifted into one half of this. We explored the other. Within were four major-generals. And two empty seats. We climbed up. 'One moment. This is a first-class compartment.'

We knew. Did we have tickets? Of course. Could they see them. No, they were ticket inspectors. So sorry; without seeing our tickets we would not be allowed to enter. The generals would see to that. And so reluctantly we departed to buy two first-class tickets from Manendru Ghat to Raxaul. And reluctantly the major-generals allowed us to rejoin them. At least we had found out where we were and where we were going. One of the generals made a great display about giving up his bench on our behalf. When the train started we found out why. It was the smuttiest bench.

The generals then devoted themselves to interrogation. A toothy one began it. 'Where are you going?' 'Where have you come from?' 'How?' 'Are you from the Peace Corps?' 'Are you students?' They could understand none of the answers. Why were we moving around India in this unkempt condition at this time of year? What was the *aim* and *object* of all this movement? Wearily we tried to explain, but the result was a failure. 'Are you on a government grant?'

For the rest of the journey they stared at us, solemnly marking down each detail for some future identification. The train jolted slowly through the night from one crowded halt to the next. The electric fans did not work. The iron bars on the windows proved useful handholds for the people outside. By the light of two dim bulbs I could make out the enormous cockroaches on the floor. It became a point of honour with me to kill any that moved. The generals were bemused by this – 'Those creatures are *totally* harmless.'

Slowly the heat melted us down; we began to feel like two half-consumed lollipops that had been dropped on a cinema floor. To boost morale we applied a liberal sprinkling of baby powder. Then we curled up on the benches and slept. Powdered lollipops sleeping like babies in a nest of generals. Nobody who smelled as we did could be really dirty. The generals sat erect in their starched British uniforms, crosslegged on their bench, brown-brogued and sockless, inscrutably looking on.

Once again the journey passed into a dream phase, only remembered through waves of tiredness and confusion. The train paused on the half-hour for half-an-hour. At each halt, one could just make out the dim forms of a packed crowd lying on the platform. Nobody stirred. The engine, whenever one went forward to inspect it, was deserted. The signal room equally so. Suddenly without warning or reason we might jolt forward again through the night. It became possible to understand Indian Railways' enormous casualty figures. On the signal-box door, there was a prettily embroidered motto: 'There is no one so deserving of praise as the careful man ...'

In the deserted stationmasters' offices were grates for a wood fire and a bank of gleaming brass levers. There were cocoa mugs stamped with the company's monogram, and a jumble of Victorian telegraphic machinery. It was as though one had been transported to a small Welsh mountain branch-line of fifty years ago. The machinery lay to hand, the domestic details were authentic, the stove had been cast in Derby. Only the will to operate the system was absent. But the relics of this impeccable plan remained to render grotesque the chaos which had succeeded. In the dark corner behind the broom cupboard one expected to see the ghost of Isambard Kingdom Brunel wringing his hands over these cunning and now misused devices. He would have felt at one with the legionaries haunting Hadrian's Wall.

Somehow during the night, stumbling across stations with unreadable names, we managed two changes. At one of these we were told that we would have to wait a few hours for the train to Raxaul. The platform was too crowded to lie on. We dragged out two kitchen chairs from the stifling heat of the stationmaster's office and slept on these. We woke at dawn. It was freezing, it was misty, slowly the recollection returned that we had spent the night on a station platform. Further down groups were lighting fires and huddling close to them. Something was wrong with the day, something was different. Rain. The first since Teheran. Stiffly we made our way down to the waiting train. We were hopeful that the last day of our journey had begun.

Beside the train there was a preliminary customs examination. Two dapper Europeans who had just arrived from Nepal were having an argument over a radio. The customs officer said that they had intended to sell it. The Europeans said that this was ridiculous, they just wanted to listen to it. The customs officer opened up the case of the younger one. Inside there was another radio, and another, and a fourth. They were

escorted away by a turbanned soldier with a twitching staff.
Where, in the Himalayas, had they got all those radios?
According to the officer, now relaxed after his triumph, it was
profitable to buy a radio in Singapore, fly it to Nepal, bring
it down to India and sell it. Customs control had only just
been tightened up on this route, and until word got round
among travellers the officer's job was money for jam. Genially
he waved through Perkins's unreceipted cameras, one arrest
a day was enough; we were ushered on to the Raxaul train and
it lurched off through the budding fields and the occasional
showers. Between dozes we watched this miracle, happily.

At Raxaul we were woken and turned off the train. It was
stiflingly hot again. There were no buses across town to the
frontier. We hitched a ride on a cart and reached a customs
post. The customs post, the last damn customs post, was closed.
A convoy of big limousines was halted outside it and from
within the hut we could hear cultured Oxford tones discussing,
disinterestedly, the regulations for importing big limousines.
No, dear boy, they had not been flown into Nepal, they had
been driven there. As for receipts, well you know how it is,
dear boy, these damn things sometimes get mislaid. No, he
could not recall any precise dates just at the moment. The
voices became more confidential for a while and then rose
again. Two impeccably-dressed Nepalese and an Indian official
finally emerged from behind the hut. Too, too tedious, old
man, but if the customs insisted on receipts then of course ...
The Nepalese clambered into their western limousines and the
westerners clambered out of their cart. The customs officer
examined us wearily. He had the air of a man who has long
since stopped trying to distinguish between the genuine Englishmen and the counterfeit ones.

Beyond the barriers, drawn up beside the dusty road, we
could see a bus. On its side in faded gold letters there was a
legend, 'Raxaul to Katmandu'. The word acted on us like a

shot, like a little yellow leapie, it was our first evidence of the promised land, the first hint that such a place might actually exist outside the fevered imaginations of those on the road. A committee of vociferous Sikhs conducted us to a bench near the back of the bus, a way was cleared through a small herd of white cows, and with hardly a sound the conveyance began to shake itself forward along the road. At least three of the Sikhs had joined the executive chain of command which was directly responsible for steering.

Our bus bounced along between dry fields towards some low hills to the north. The track ran straight on, the committee were conducting us at a furious pace, and for a while there was nothing to distinguish the blurred landscape from the India we had officially left. Then suddenly the trail disappeared into a thick rain forest. Without any slackening of pace the bus whizzed into the dense greenery, the path turned from dust to mud, great tree trunks caused intricate diversions, in every clearing we expected to see at least one tiger ... Once we did catch a glimpse of something large and brightly coloured moving behind the leaves. A clearing showed it to be the down bus making its own way home. In the middle of this jungle the track sank into a series of potholes big enough to drown an elephant. The Sikhs bounded in and out of them at full speed. Opposite two of the Nepalese passengers had taken to lying on the floor. After a while, when the committee had soaked themselves, their guests and the luggage on the roof, we struggled out of the forest and started to climb.

Towards midday we stopped for lunch at a dank hut perched on a small plateau above a torrent. A party of Hindu pilgrims were completing their meal, dark men from the south with fierce eyes and matted hair. They had travelled a thousand miles up the length of the sub-continent to visit a remote valley in the mountains whose streams fed the Ganges. They were already excited that their journey was so nearly complete.

After the meal, sitting under the high stone bridge which spanned the torrent, half-hidden among the boulders, bathing in the spray, I felt a hand plucking my sleeve. It was one of the pilgrims, his face only a few inches from mine, his wild eye beaming through mine. I must excuse him, but was I by any chance acquainted with the Duke of Wellington? A pity – back in Colombo there was a young relative of His Grace visiting their house. So nice to have met me. He disappeared among the rocks and we resumed our separate journeys.

After the parched heat of the Ganges valley the pass over the Himalayan foothills was an uncanny place. Looking down into the clouded gorges, we felt we were flying rather than riding in a bus, so impossible did it seem that anyone should build a road among these crags. Late in the afternoon we passed a corner called Everest Point and began to descend. As we dropped through the clouds they dispersed and the sun came out, and we saw spread below us a valley that was unlike any other place we had seen.

Everywhere there were terraced fields sparkling in the evening light, the springing rice was divided by vivid green banks, and clear streams tinkled over them and swept into lush water meadows below. There were butterflies and swallows and wagtails, women worked and children played in the lush wetness of it all, and in the narrow cuts which linked the ripe valleys were lanes overhung with banyan trees, and leathery water buffalo were browsing in the hedges. We could not get accustomed to the water. It ran over the land in an astonishing profusion, delicately colouring the earth's hard face, and washing away our memories of its formerly cracked skin. At the day's end we reached a police post situated in a leafy grove. The policemen were dozing in the grass, but they rose to welcome our bus to their kingdom, and they gravely presented us with little badges bearing their King's head. We pinned these on, and wore them like charms. They were alerions, the eagle without beak or claws, the benevolent ruler, the badge of the good Prince.

Katmandu was just down the road. In the dusk it was a big village, wood smoke rising from the roofs of its exquisite carved houses, children dancing round our bus for the honour and profit of leading us to lodgings. The Sikhs were immediately asleep on their back benches, the rest of the passengers speedily dispersed about their ways. Sitting on the ground in the gloom across the road, under the wall of the post office, we could make out a familiar figure. It was Rat and he looked at ease.

Rat was staying in a tiny communal room at 307 Maruhity – or the Camp Hotel as his host insisted on calling it – behind Ganesh Sthan Temple. It was a wooden house, delicately joined, following the most exacting medieval principles, and fashioned according to the traditional dimensions. That is to say none of us could stand up inside. It was Rat's temporary headquarters: temporary because he was fixing up more comfortable accommodation in a house just outside the village in a few days. The house had been taken by some of his former acquaintance from the Gulhane, and at this end of the road Rat found them remarkably improved. He was relaxing now, accustoming himself to the feeling that there was nowhere he had to go today, or tomorrow, or the next day: that his journey was complete, the pursuit evaded and it was time to rest.

There were a number of curiosities in the village to divert Rat while he grew used to his peace. In the narrow streets beneath the towering wooden pagodas were the stalls of the Nepalese markets. Spices were sold, and trinkets and vegetables, and hash. The nearest hash vendor was always within signalling distance, and he sold nothing but the best black goods, rolled into a shiny egg, a heavy week's supply for a few shillings. Only one of the stallholders was not Nepalese. He was an old pale man squatting on a plank like a monkey, dressed in the usual white robes, and selling matches. His skin and his eyes were grey, his bones long and heavy and he had a scrawny beard. But he talked to no one, he cultivated his mystery, and Rat had to conclude that he was either a genetic throwback or the grandfather of the white saddhus. The old man was not telling which in any European language at all.

Outside Katmandu on the road to the west of the country was a shrine to the all seeing eye of Buddha. It was here at the Bodh Nath Stupa that some of the Tibetan monks who had fled in 1959 had set up their headquarters. Most of their leaders had gone on to India to join the Dalai Lama, but one at least had stayed right here in the Bodh Nath to help his people. He was the Cheney Lama and one could seek an audience with him in his little house at one side of the court which surrounded the great four-eyed dome of the Stupa. On the door of his house there was a notice 'Conservation and Development Committee'; for Cheney had become a commercial lama. The wisdom which guaranteed survival was no longer to be found in the dictates of the Lord Buddha or in teaching one's brothers how to live in peace. It was a matter of farm prices now, and how much could be raised on the sale of a sacred ikon, a *tanka*, and whether any of his people could learn a trade. This was not why Rat came out to Bodh Nath Stupa – he was more interested in the lama's other speciality. These were hard times and it was usually a matter of some hours waiting on the shady side of the court, crouched beneath the nearest of the Lord Buddha's all seeing eyes, fending off the pie dogs, ignoring the pleading looks of the children's band, before the friendly lama could lay aside the cares of the grain deficit and give Rat fifteen minutes on the dissenting errors of *Srijunga Dewangsi*. The Lord Buddha had to wait his turn: He was Comrade Buddha now.

If Rat did not feel up to the trek to Bodh Nath, he passed

the time lying around in the park of one of the great hotels, sheltered from the showers by their fruit trees, dozing the day away. On the lawns of the Royal Hotel he might get an hour or two undisturbed before Ma Scott, who was the proprietor's mother-in-law, saw him and set the ponies loose. Sometimes a party of Tibetan tramps would come scuttling down the drive, squat men in leather aprons, .their pigtails smeared with buffalo butter, having failed to sell sacred tankas or brass chastity belts to Ma Scott – another of the Cheney Lama's schemes going awry.

Further along the road, in the Annapurna Hotel, Rat would get even shorter shrift. The Annapurna was the grandest hotel in Katmandu. It was owned by the King's sister and was built in ferro-concrete. Unfortunately it was not doing the business it might have been since the foundations had sunk on one side and all the lifts had swung out of true. But the doorman was still quite nifty. Once, after being chased down the road, Rat met a guest of the Annapurna. He was an oldish man, French, and he said he was looking for his daughter. He had come to Katmandu all the way from Valenciennes to find her and to take her home. He had paid all her debts and the debts of her friends – and now she would not come. He showed Rat the concentration camp stencil on his arm, and sat by the side of the road, and wept.

His daughter had good reason for not taking the first plane back to Valenciennes. Right at that moment she was sitting in the front room of a pretty little house at 10/603 Bhotahity talking to Australian John and waiting for methedrine and the Doc. The Doc, or Doctor Akhanda Prasad Pradhan to give him his full style and dignity, was a little old Nepalese with a pot belly and an obscenely unwrinkled skin and a pretty wife. His supplies of heroin and cocaine had so far proved inexhaustible. According to the label on his bottles the Doc's supplies came from Burgoyne, Burbridge & Co. Ltd., a firm long-established in East Ham, but Akhanda did not charge East Ham prices. A bottle of pure liquid heroin cost only six hundred rupees, or you could buy it by the shot at twelve rupees – ten shillings. John had come for his morning fix and he was in none too good a mood about it. 'You got me on this stuff Doc,' he said, 'Now you can get me off again.' The Doc smiled serenely, waxily and made no reply. The Australian was one of his best customers just then, and anyway he had no pethidine.

The Doc would sit behind his little wooden desk for hours chatting to the customers and drinking the tea which his wife brought down to him at regular intervals. He would talk of gold prices in India, and hash prices in London, and courier routes and the seasons. He would talk of almost any subject he could think of, but he did not like to hear mention of Werner. If you mentioned Werner the Doc's glossy little dial would cloud over, and some of the sunshine would go out of his life and he might even shed a glycerine tear or two. Werner was dead. He had died the week before up at the Shanta Bhawar Mission Hospital, of hepatitis.

The doctors up at the hospital said that Werner had been admitted in the last stages of an hepatic coma, that he was a heroin addict who they had had to put under heavy sedation when he attacked one of the Nepalese nurses during a violent withdrawal syndrome, and that when he was under sedation some of his friends had slipped him L.S.D. which had killed him.

His friends said that he was a heroin addict who had been over-sedated by the hospital, that there had been no L.S.D. in the valley at that time, and that even when he became seriously ill he could have been saved if the German Embassy had agreed to supply the hospital with the hopelessly expensive gamma globulin which they were keeping for their own staff.

The German Embassy had no comment to make about the causes of Werner's death but agreed that they had arranged for his cremation without an inquest. One could not even visit Werner's grave, since he had been cremated on the communal fire behind the mortuary.

Despite the rumours about the gamma globulin Rat was fond of the Shanta Bhawar. To get there you took a bus out into the green lanes to the north of the village, and after winding down these for a while you came to a high wall and a fine gateway and behind that a fine stone house. In the carriageway sat the Nepalese families waiting to visit a relative. They squatted together in tight groups, preparing food over fires and watching their children play. Some of the families had not come there to visit a relative at all, but had come to be vaccinated against smallpox. Whole families came at a time, but after they arrived at the gates it was a few days before they ventured inside. It was after all an honour to be visited by the smallpox god; if you survived his visit he left the scars as a sign that you had a special mission in life, and since he was patently a powerful god, and might resent this rather ungracious closing of the door in his face, the Nepalese spent some time in placatory sacrifices before submitting to the innoculation. Like Orwell's cook in Paris, who was only allowed three candles to work with, and said that three were unlucky and carried on with two, the Nepalese outside the hospital seemed determined to double their already heavy burden.

Inside the hospital Rat usually found a few friends to pass the time with. There was May, a pretty girl from Connecticut who had been taken in with measles, which in Nepal is a plague killing many thousands of people a year. May was in a cool white side-ward behind a delicate mosquito net and was generally grateful for the fuss they made of her. It was a mission hospital and they asked her to pay what money she could since most of the Nepalese could pay nothing. This seemed fair, so May asked her friend Richard who had brought her in and who had all the money. But Richard just stood by her bed, looked out of the window at the families in the drive, murmured something about 'all the groovy ones are brahmins', and didn't give her a penny. He had plans for May when she came out of hospital. He was going to fly her home to Connecticut with a very great deal of hash, and she was going to send him the money. He had it all worked out. A few days later May was discharged, in tears, without paying anything and taken away by Richard. He was back a few days after that, with measles, and this time he did pay.

Further along the corridor there was a hepatitis case. Visiting was only allowed reluctantly. Nicole would be in that little room for maybe three months. She had no friends left in the valley, they had all slipped away to Europe, and Nicole was a vivid yellow colour and very bored and lonely. Rat visited her once, and Nicole became quite affectionate and offered Rat a drink and a cuddle and biscuit. But Rat did not fancy that yellow colour and had just had a meal. After he left Nicole he asked a nurse what the bowl outside contained and the nurse said it was disinfectant and that Rat must wash his hands in it after visiting, even if he had touched nothing, hepatitis was that contagious. This was a fact which Nicole knew very well when she handed Rat the drink and the biscuit. She could have done with a bit of company.

Then there was Jonathan. He had been in the valley for some months now and it was proving to be too long. He was getting morbid, spending too much time on his own, brooding and hanging around the Hindu cremations. Jonathan had taken to begging for his living, and he spent most of his time begging off the other overlanders. He could not get a room in the cheapest doss house anymore. Instead he had to sleep in the open, under a pagoda roof if he was lucky, or just under the sky. Jonathan had not found paradise in the valley.

His journey had been a circular one, he had peeled off the outer layers of the distance that separated him from escape, and he was back where he had started. The same defeated face was in the mirror, the same filth surrounded him, the same people told him no. Everywhere he went Jonathan found endless reflections of someone he had met last month or would meet tomorrow.

That was why he had come out here, he thought. To separate himself from the herd he was a fragment of, to chip an identity for himself out of the cold isolation of the mountains. And so he found his flight futile. There were as many of him here as there were anywhere else. He could not even die.

Just down the road, past the royal palace where the flies drowsed noisily on the hash plants under the wall, was the Consul's office, and should there be any immediate danger of Jonathan dying, this man would speedily loan him an air ticket back to England. Jonathan had come all this way and found at the end of his flight that the organisation which he had abandoned so scornfully had a representative awaiting his inevitable call. They had not even bothered to pursue him; they were already installed in an unobtrusive corner of his last refuge. His had been a pilgrimage to a vice-consul; the only god he found in the mountain kingdom was an official one. One day the god gave him an air ticket home.

This was the kingdom which Rat discovered to us in the days after our arrival. It was his playground and he took his ease. And when he had tired of playing, Rat had other plans. He only spoke of them in a low voice, and preferably after dark, and then again when there was no one around: when his luck was in and the Furies might not overhear, that was when he spoke of Paradise.

If you walked to the eastern end of the village, under the black pagodas, past the barber on the temple steps, down the lane to the shallow swift river which was the home of a God you came to the Hindu funeral ground. If you trotted past the corpse waiting to be burned, trying not to see the wrinkled, brown leg stump erect in the ashes, returned the greetings of the men who stoked the bonfire and crossed the rope bridge, looking down through the slats at the water-sleeked backs of the water-buffalo asleep in the stream, you found, as like as not, that you were being greeted by Mr Singh.

Mr Singh wore a three-piece pin-stripe made in Calcutta and a tattered white turban. He was rightly named, for his voice was high and sweet and he pitched it all over the place in just one sentence. 'You alone?' said Mr Singh, 'lonely? Mr Singh tell you all the future. Tell you all the past. All about your girl. Your troubles. Mr Singh tell.' And if you slipped him a small coin fairly frequently he would too. He sang it all shrewdly and without too many mistakes, and softly enough to make you feel quite uncomfortable if you had not been feeling so already. He sat on the steps of a little stone temple on the far bank of the river, no one in sight, just the backs and noses of the water buffalo, and the rushing water, with the fish jumping and his high-pitched voice in the wind. When he had finished, Mr Singh would always suggest another appointment, because there was always more to tell. Tomorrow? No, not tomorrow, because then he had to see the King.

And surprisingly enough that was also true. King Mahendra Bir Bikram Shah Deva (the second) was the inventor of the Panchyat system of democracy, the only system of democracy which relied for its foundation on the sole decision of one man, the King; he was also very superstitious, and he consulted the soothsayers daily. Mr Singh was one of his favourites, and the old man took his stones and bones and ribbons and stump of pencil into the palace almost every week.

The King needed advice: his country was after all next on the list to Tibet so far as the gentlemen in Peking were concerned; it was poor, it was decentralised, it was defenceless. It relied on American aid, but when the American Vice-President paid a visit riots broke out. It was a bastion of democratic freedom, but it was not unusual for a deposed Prime Minister to spend a year or so in jail, and, according to the men who knew these things, it was one of the eleven worst countries in the world for repressing trade unions – ranking with Russia and Greece and Spain and South Africa.

And above all there was the big red brother whose fraternal hug could be so stifling. King Mahendra's country was full of the victims of this affection, and they counted themselves, homeless as they were, the lucky ones. The story now told in the Blue Tibetan Inn, by its refugee proprietor, was that the Chinese were cutting off the legs of any Tibetans found trying to cross the border. Only the warrior Kampas still resisted them, and they were armed with no more than clubs.

His Majesty maintained that the Chinese were his good friends, and among the most trusted of his allies, and they would as soon be invading his country as he would be invading theirs. He was heard to say this fairly often most days of his life. And he still consulted soothsayers.

Possibly these wise men had had something to do with the King's latest scheme to beat the Chinese. High up on the border with Tibet there was a road which led from Lhasa to Katmandu. (It was the first time that a serviceable road had linked the two countries, the Chinese had built it, and there was a greatly exaggerated rumour that it was strong enough to bear the weight of a tank.) At Kodari, the last place along this road in Nepal, the King had caused to be erected a giant portrait of himself which stared out across 'Friendship Bridge' at a similar depiction of the Great Red Chairman himself. Beneath the King's picture were inscribed various of the Royal sayings. He was after all the philosopher King, his courtiers said so and wrote pamphlets about his wisdom with such titles as *Understanding His Majesty – in a Nutshell*; so there was no shortage of sayings to inscribe – 'Education is the life-blood of a nation' for example, or 'Student polemics are gruesome' or one of the King's favourites, 'Do not imitate others in things that are beyond your means.'

Far below this soundless confrontation, other preparations were being made. On a dry afternoon anyone walking over the fields around the villages might hear the distinct high chatter of a Mark 1 Bren and, passing through a few trees, would come across a well-drilled detachment firing one. The soldiers were conscientious men, immaculately dressed and meticulous in the care of their ancient weaponry. They were waiting, that was clear. But nobody would say who they were preparing for. One thing was certain, it was nothing at all to do with the Chinese. And pending the solution of this mystery, Mahendra could continue to act out his role as the Alerion. He was the clawless eagle, the mythological creature only believed in by a quiescent peasantry. Ask any Nepalese trade unionist.

Of course Rat did not ask, nor did he consider the Bren gun practice, or the road to Lhasa or the Chinese news library : his thoughts were fixed on Paradise.

Leaving Mr Singh, he would go up the steep path on the river's far bank and through several small hamlets where, in the open rooms, he could see the primitive machinery for bottling the coloured sugar which passed for coca-cola in some parts of town. Climbing steadily through the woods beyond a clearing above the highest hamlet, he looked for the stone steps.

The trees were tall and leafy and grew wonderfully close together, as trees should which hide the steps to Paradise. If you searched long enough they sprang apart suddenly to reveal a towering Buddha, the stone Buddha in red robes and yellow skin, with kohl on his eyelids and rings in his ears. He sat straight-backed and cross-legged, with one hand careless on his knee, resting on the dull grey stones and the polished black stones of his seat. In the rock behind him were niches filled with statues, and in other clearings, behind the tangled trees, other Buddhas could be seen. They were the guardians of this hill, but the steps wound up invitingly between them, and so Rat paid whatever tribute his superstition owed, and continued to climb.

Up and up through the trees, and towards the tip of light that glinted and winked above; the steps grew steeper and narrower and the trees crept closer in. And as he climbed he clung to the rope at the side and made it leap for yards ahead, and suddenly from ahead of him up the hill would come a scrambling and a chattering and a rushing, and down the rope came monkeys, the second guardians of the sanctuary. Tribute to these had to be paid in kind rather than in prayer; no one approached the shrine who was not bearing gifts.

At the top of the stairs the trees gave way to a crumbling stone wall, and the staircase, almost vertical by now, disappeared into a slit. The monkeys would not try this passage; they left Rat and scaled the wall to some entrance of their own. Rat climbed on, through the shade of the cut, beneath a low roof and out into the blinding light of the platform above. Here the sun was no longer broken by the trees, it was reflected directly from the white dome of the shrine and from the turrets around it. This was a fortress as well as a temple and from its parapets Rat could look far across the valley. He could count the three villages of the capital, he could count the rivers, and the water-buffalo and the pagodas. The forests and the mountains were beneath him. His hair danced in the wind like a flag, and he looked down on the roof of the world.

Inside the walls were many rooms, and the monkeys and the dogs ran freely among the chapels and the altars and the places of rest. In one room an old man was tended by two disciples. They lifted him and dressed him and turned him, they shared out their food, and he blessed them. Elsewhere another pilgrim sat alone. He was filthy and abandoned and half-starved, and he could not communicate with this community. He knew nothing of them, or why they were there. He knew nothing and he did not care. He had scented the holiness of this place; it was what he had come for. He knew a shrine when he got inside one. It was cold in the stone room, he shivered and was hungry. On his wrist was a cut where that morning a monkey had bitten him. Was it rabid? Could you die from the bite of a sacred monkey? Should he wash and bind it? For the time being he would not; he would just sit and be holy; he was in a shrine. Inside that little stone room, inside that little starved head was Theseus, half the son of a god. And thankfully, now that he had come this far, now that he had hidden himself so well, nobody was going to argue about it.

And Rat, looking in on his silence, could stop running at last. Though this man was a stranger, he was not afraid. On the damp stone before him, rapt in the discovery of its own existence, sat the child that he had been.

A choir chanted, a dog barked, a bell rang. Though the chamber beside him was empty, a light voice sang within. On a clear day in Paradise the stones as well will sing.